North Carolina
REFLECTIONS OF 400 YEARS

COMMISSIONED BY BB&T

NorthCarolina
REFLECTIONS OF 400 YEARS

COMMISSIONED BY BB&T

JCP CORP.

Library of Congress Catalog Number 84-80302
ISBN 0-938694-15-4

Epley Associates, Inc.
P.O. Box 1801
Raleigh, North Carolina 27602

Overall Project Coordination
by Epley Associates, Inc., Public Relations

Book Design by W. Bradley Miller

Photographic Coordination by Chip Henderson

Printed by Stephenson, Inc.

DUST JACKET: The Blue Ridge Mountains, seven
miles north of Boone, on the Blue Ridge Parkway.
Photography by Chip Henderson.

Contents

How well the past leads us
to understand . . .
what mothers teach in whispers
and fathers with a shout,
to become . . .
a mind and heart molded
by history's touch
and shaped by the land,
to walk . . .
shimmering into the future.

INTRODUCTION

It is my pleasure and great pride to present this book, *North Carolina: Reflections of 400 Years,* which we at BB&T offer to the people of North Carolina in honor of America's 400th anniversary celebration.

BB&T was founded in 1872 in Wilson by Alpheus T. Branch, after whom Branch Banking and Trust Company was named. Because of our unique status as North Carolina's oldest bank, BB&T shares in the keen awareness of our heritage as the home of the first English settlement in the New World.

Our heritage is much more than a series of events deemed important from the perspective of the present. It is a progression of knowledge from generation to generation, molded by the wisdom and example of those who have lived before us and passed down from parent to child.

North Carolina's Museum of History is a repository of that wisdom and example, and as chairman of the fund-raising drive for a new home for the Museum, I am pleased that a percentage

of the proceeds from the sale of this book will benefit this worthy cause.

It is the land that most significantly affects our heritage, and North Carolina's terrain has created a variety of lifestyles and customs. Safe harbors and sandy beaches breed a love of the untamed and the spirit of adventure; the fertile earth develops an appreciation for the land and artistic expression; lofty heights produce a ruggedness and the will to endure.

It is now our opportunity to build upon our inheritance, to retain North Carolina's position as a leader while we search for new shores to claim, new lands to till, new mountains to scale.

If our past is any indication of our future, our children and their children will continue to reflect the unique spirit and character that is North Carolina. BB&T is proud to be a part of that spirit.

L. Vincent Lowe, Jr.
President and
Chief Executive Officer
BB&T

Land of Beginnings

CHAPTER 1

INTRODUCTION TO CHAPTER 1
BY TOM MASSENGALE

An enthusiastic hiker and dedicated conservationist, Thomas Massengale is director/vice-president of the southeast regional office of the Nature Conservancy in Chapel Hill. He holds an undergraduate degree in history from The University of North Carolina at Chapel Hill and a master's degree in landscape architecture from North Carolina State University.

We came to Carolina four centuries ago seeking treasure, and we found it.

There was gold in the evening sun setting across the tawny sands and miles of marsh of our coastal islands from Currituck to Calabash, and silver in the moonlight awash over the great inland seas of Albemarle and Pamlico.

We ventured west, up the rivers to the fall line, along the Indian trading paths, amazed each step of the way at all the rich and varied lands that belonged to our one province: the great cypress and gum swamps, and the broad forested plains stretching over the east; the rich river bottoms and rolling hills beyond; and the pinnacles and ranges in the central province that foretold the higher hills, the blue ridge and all the great blue-misted mountains to come.

From Neuse River to Newfound Gap, from Bald Head Island to Bluff Mountain, we found treasure in our terrain.

We were amazed anew at all the wild and diverse life of this land, its birds and fish, its otters and cougars and bear, its pines and palmettoes in the east and its balsam firs in the west, its thousands of wildflowers jeweling the countryside at every turn.

How have we done by this treasure over the course of twenty generations?

Some of it we have squandered, but most of it we have spent well, investing and banking it in a wide variety of productive ways: in crop and livestock farms, in towns and cities, in lakes for reservoirs and power and in lands for manufacturers. We have re-created that original trove, made of it wealth from earth and industry, a wealth of opportunity and a wealth of character.

It is our character, as a people with an abiding love for our lands and waters, that makes us willing stewards of North Carolina. And as such, we have set aside

many of our finest natural lands — perhaps one acre out of a hundred — in parks and forests, in refuges and preserves. There is still more for us to do, and our time is short. For what we have saved and what we will save in the very near future will be all that remains of this great treasure for our children and our children's children.

And we guard this treasure not only to remember the source of our wealth, but also to keep about us the very sources of our natural and spiritual well-being.

In tempest and at peace, the Atlantic Ocean has drawn North Carolinians and visitors from throughout the world to marvel at its beauty, enjoy its diversions and benefit from its bounty.

The Outer Banks, a unique island string, lie as pearls around the neck of North Carolina's eastern coast, the furthest point east in the continental United States.

Cape Lookout National Seashore comprises the southern portion of this natural barrier island system and offers 58 miles of undisturbed beach accessible only by boat.

Greenfield Gardens, a municipal park in Wilmington, blossoms with extensive plantings of azaleas and other flowers indigenous to North Carolina. The five mile drive around Greenfield Lake is a highlight of the annual Azalea Festival, which attracts thousands of visitors each spring.

14

Canoeists at Merchants Millpond State Park in Gates County quietly glide through the placid waters, shaded by bald cypress trees festooned with Spanish moss. A winter stopover for migrating waterfowl, the park claims the oldest and largest stand of bald cypress in North Carolina.

Smith Island, also known as Bald Head Island for the development now there, provides the best nesting habitat known in North Carolina for the loggerhead turtle. The state's only subtropical island complex, it harbors one of the largest remaining live oak forests. "Old Baldy," the famous lighthouse, is located near the island boat landing.

Lake Mattamuskeet is the largest natural lake in North Carolina. Located in Hyde County, it is famous as a waterfowl refuge and hunting area.

Jockey's Ridge is considered the largest natural sand dune on the east coast of the United States, and is ranked among the highest dunes in the world. Located on Bodie Island, just north of Nags Head on the Outer Banks, Jockey's Ridge state park borders the 1,900 acre Nags Head Woods maritime forest.

A treasure for beachcombers, a souvenir for a small child, raw material for the artist, all are in search for the perfect shell.

The fabric of North Carolina's Piedmont is an intricate lace work of small ponds and farmers' fields, water reeds and rolling landscape, misty horizons and fragrant blossoms.

Found scattered within many southeastern counties are shallow, pond-like depressions ranging in size from a few acres to more than one thousand. They provide a habitat for many rare animals and plants. Some, like Goose Pond and Pretty Pond in Robeson County, are among the rarest unprotected ecosystems in the United States.

Approaching the vistas to the west, peach and apple orchards dot the landscape and provide not only visions of springtime color but important elements in the economic fabric of the state.

The history and lives of North Carolinians for more than 400 years are interwoven with its farms. This rural heritage has influenced the state's government, economy and education. Without a dominant major city, hundreds of smaller towns have sprung up, almost everywhere that plowed fields end and people need to meet.

One of eight national natural landmarks in North Carolina, Green Swamp in Brunswick County, is host to numerous wildflowers and various species of insect-eating plants, including the Venus fly trap and the yellow pitcher. The swamp is also one of the few sanctuaries for the black bear, red-cockaded woodpecker and the American alligator.

Autumn's chorus of vivid color in North Carolina is a breathtaking experience. A leisurely tour on the Blue Ridge Parkway, America's most popular scenic drive, rivals the color and pageantry of the best Saturday football game, as thousands step into nature's dream of greens, golds, reds and yellows.

Even after the brilliant glory of a fall festival, the now naked trees exhibit a stark beauty as they prepare for winter's chill and swirling snows. "Good timber does not grow in ease," the poet has said. "For the stronger the wind, the tougher the trees."

25

The roar of sparkling waters as they rush to an unseen destination has fascinated mankind for generations. Like children, these special treasures of nature are named and cherished. Cullasaja Falls, near Franklin, is one of North Carolina's highest, cascading almost 250 feet.

Other waterfalls located in the mountainous western part of the state include Hickory Nut Falls at Chimney Rock, Linville Falls in the Pisgah National Forest and Whitewater Falls, near Oakland in Transylvania County, believed to be the highest in eastern America at 411 feet.

The Joyce Kilmer Memorial Forest, near Robbinsville, along with Slickrock Wilderness, is part of the Nantahala National Forest. Together they form a fitting memorial to the author of "Trees."

This 14,000 acre wilderness provides the adventurous with a landscape of virgin forest, sparkling water and flowering shrubs. The forest borders the Great Smoky Mountains National Park, America's most visited national park.

Northeast of the park, at Deep Gap near Asheville, Mt. Mitchell, eastern America's highest point, offers a panoramic view from 6,684 feet, part of a nearly 1,500-acre state park.

Pisgah National Forest, is part of the more than 1.1 million acres of national forests in North Carolina. Considered the cradle of forestry science, it was in the Pisgah National Forest near Black Mountain in Transylvania County that forestry was first taught and practiced in 1898.

It looks for all the world as if a piece of the "far North" has taken up residence in North Carolina. The spruce and fir tree forest in Mt. Mitchell State Park is a disjunct population of plants naturally found in Canada. The heavy foliage gives even a sunny May afternoon a special feeling usually reserved for dusk.

A range of the Appalachian system, the Blue Ridge mountains run through five states. People who preserve the "old ways" of life and speech still call its remote valleys "home."

Loves and Lifestyles

CHAPTER 2

A Fine Frenzy of Singing Birds

BY SAM RAGAN

Some months ago, Terry Sanford, our former governor and now president of Duke University, came across an article in a newspaper in which Dr. Karl Menninger, the father of American psychiatry, was quoted as saying he had stopped his regular practice and now spent his time visiting patients and reading poetry to them. He found poetry to be of great therapeutic value for the patients.

Sanford penned the following verse and sent it along with the clipping:

Hail to poets,
Your day has come,
Your work beats valium,
To say nothing of rum.

Sanford spoke truthfully, because whether as therapy, literature, aesthetics or art, poetry has come into its own in North Carolina.

Early in this century, John Charles McNeill attained a measure of popularity with his verse, some of it in dialect, written out of the cottonfields and creeks and woods of his native Scotland County. But there were few other poets who came along to take up his calling, and a quarter-century ago, the number of practicing poets in North Carolina could be counted on the fingers of the hands.

Today, however, if an anthology of the best of North Carolina poetry were to be published, more than one hundred poets would have to be represented in such a work.

This burgeoning of poetry and what was described in the Elizabethan Age as "a fine frenzy of singing birds" can be attributed to several causes, chief of which was the development in the state of a large number of first-rate literary magazines. Poets have found a place to be published in such excellent publications as "Crucible" at Atlantic Christian College, "St. Andrews Review" at St. Andrews Presbyterian College, "Pembroke Magazine" at Pembroke State University, "Miscellany" at Davidson College, "Carolina Quarterly" at Chapel Hill, the "Greensboro Review," the "Lyricist" at Campbell University, and the "Southern Poetry Review" founded by Guy Owen and now published at the University of North Carolina at Charlotte.

The North Carolina Arts Council was the catalytic force behind the magazines and the burgeoning of poetry. The Council awarded small grants to the magazines, and it sponsored poetry readings across the state as well as the first statewide poetry-in-the-school program. All of these encouraged the writing and reading of poetry and helped create a climate favorable for this art form.

Recently, at the Weymouth Center for the Arts and Humanities in Southern Pines, more than one hundred fifty poets turned out for the Fifth Annual North Carolina Poetry Festival, and all of them read at the all-day event.

Several small publishing houses have been established and in recent years have published dozens of volumes of poetry. Among them are Blair and Jackpine Press of Winston-Salem, St. Andrews of Laurinburg, Carolina Wren Press of Carrboro, Briarpatch Press of Davidson, and formerly Moore Publishing Company of Durham and Red Clay Press, founded by Charleen Whisnant, in Charlotte.

Many North Carolina poets have won national recognition for their work—Randall Jarrell, A.R. Ammons and Fred Chappell among them—and among the poets who have received high critical praise for their poetry are Betty Adcock, Heather Ross Miller, Shelby Stephenson, Stephen Smith, Agnes McDonald, Mary Snotherly, Shirley Moody, James Applewhite, Paul Jones, Ann Deagon, Emily Wilson, Guy Owen, Thomas Walters, Thad Stem Jr., Ann Dunn, Grace DiSantos, Julie Suk, Ronald Bayes, Grace Gibson, John Foster West, Reynolds Price, Mae Woods Bell, Harriet Doar, Jean Morgan, Robert Grey, Ardis Kimzey, Sally Buckner, Michael McFee, Sallie Nixon, Virginia Love Long,

Marie Gilbert, Mary Belle Campbell, Margaret Baddour, and the list could go on and on.

Each of these poets is an individual voice, belonging to no poetic "school" but writing out of their own experience, their time and place. There is a Tar Heel flavor in many of their poems, but their art transcends all boundaries save those of the human spirit.

Poetry, indeed, flourishes in North Carolina.

A Journey With Poetry

Poetry to me is the distilled essence of an experience, a feeling, and a poem is the embodiment of all the arts—movement as in the dance, music and rhythm, a visual image and sculpted in form. Poems are about places as well as people, and North Carolina is the place of most of my poems.

These poems are part of a journey across North Carolina—from the coast to the mountains—and each seeks to freeze a moment in time in a special place.

The reader of poetry is as important as the poet himself; each must bring imagination to the experience. We invite the reader to join us in this journey and this experience.

North Carolina's Poet Laureate, Ragan is a long time resident of Southern Pines where he is Editor and Publisher of *The Pilot*. In addition to a recently published collection of his works entitled "Journey Into Morning," he is the author of two previously published prize winning collections, "To The Water's Edge" and "The Tree In The Far Pasture."

A Walk On The Beach

On the beach
The birds go walking —
Ahead of me in my walking.
With each wave a feeding,
A movement to the water's edge,
And then away,
Always away, always returning,
Even as I return
To the water's edge.
But I reach a point of turning back.
The birds go on.

—From To The Water's Edge.

Gray Horizons

Sometimes the birds pause in flight
To feed upon the foam-beaten sands,
But more often they wheel and cry
Far overhead, never stopping, until night's
Soft crescendo of silence
Calls them home.

The beach is a lonely place
On days like this,
And eyes see far until
The place where sea meets sky
Brings vision back again
To the glitter and cry
Of flashing sea gulls.

And here is the haven of
Life's mute testimonials—
A broken oar, a battered box,
And here the wreckage of some
Mist-shrouded Odyssey.
They tell no tales, except silence:
The story is your own.

—From The Tree In The Far Pasture.

Sandhills Summer

They say the sea was once here,
And sometimes at night
When the wind is rising
I can hear the sea's surge
In the sound of the pines.

You have gathered the brown branches
Which bear the pink blossoms
And I watch you arrange them
In a green bowl.
Your hands ask questions
And then give the answers.

It is very still tonight,
Before morning there will be rain.
The only sound is the cry of the cat
Wanting to come in.

I sleep under the shadow of ghost winds.

—From Journey Into Morning.

The Monument On The Capitol Grounds

He leans forward, gun in hand,
Stone eyes staring, forelock falling
Over forehead on which a pigeon sat.
    First to fall at Bethel,
    The stone words say...
But that was long ago
In a little churchyard
Where bullets whined, and where
A dog now whimpers
On a rabbit's path.
    And in the square azaleas bloom,
    A girl comes walking...
    The stone soldier stares.
    He does not hear the mockingbird's cry.

—From The Tree In The Far Pasture.

38

Postwar

He came home from Petersburg,
Footing it down the road with three others
Who fell off by the way,
He going the last miles alone.
The chimney's smoke quickened his steps.
She was waiting in the doorway
And ran down the path to meet him.
Not much was said:
They walked back together
And he took off his hat and stood a moment
Before going in to supper.

He cleaned the spring,
And there were three places
   in the fence to mend.
A new ground was cleared,
And after the plowing was done,
Along the road he planted a row of cedars.

—From The Tree In The Far Pasture.

The Apple Man

The apple stand stood close by the road,
And the apples we bought from the basket
He tested in his hands,
Rubbing them until they caught
The sun's glance and gleam.
He had grown them himself,
He wanted them to look their best.

—From Journey Into Morning.

I Watched October

I watched October
Flare today.
The flames spread along the highway,
Across the ridges, along the creek banks
Where sycamores marched naked.
October raced before me,
   red and yellow, orange,
And the purple of sweetgum.
I traveled through the sun
Into the night's silences,
Marking the moment of no consequence,
Stapling it down for keeps.
I feel it burning, the last hurrah—
Who tends the ovens of October?

—From Journey Into Morning.

A Moment In Time When The Whole World Was Blue

A lone butterfly
Came to the crevice
Where a flower grew.
Poised there on the side of the mountain,
Blue wings between
Blue flowers,
Blue sky.

—From To The Water's Edge.

Pride in Preservation

BY DR. WILLIAM S. PRICE, JR.

At the turn of this century, various leaders in politics, business and industry in North Carolina made a conscious decision to preserve and promote the historic resources of their state. By 1900, many Tar Heels wanted to declare to the rest of the country that they had emerged from the defeat of the Civil War (thirty-five years earlier) as a part of a "New South." In order to proclaim the vitality and vigor of this new image, they chose to concentrate much of their attention on the virtues of the Old South. If they could demonstrate the greatness of their past, they would legitimize a claim to future greatness.

In 1903, the North Carolina General Assembly established the state Historical Commission (the third oldest such state institution in the country) and charged that body with preserving the history of the state and presenting it to its citizens and to the world. Such preservation and presentation would take a variety of forms, including conserving archives, mounting museum exhibitions, printing historical publications and preserving historic sites and structures.

Today, historic preservation is a term that is nearly exclusively associated with the restoration and rehabilitation of historic structures. That name identification began most strongly with passage by the United States Congress in 1949 of the act establishing the National Trust for Historic Preservation and was solidified in 1966 with passage of the National Historic Preservation Act.

Tar Heels were involved in these early national efforts. People like Gordon Gray, Christopher Crittenden, Robert Stipe, Gertrude Carraway and Banks Talley have been figures of major importance on the national preservation scene, but they all "cut their teeth" on the rich resources of North Carolina.

Historic preservation in North Carolina has involved a unique partnership between state and local government and the private sector. The state currently owns and operates through its Division of Archives and History twenty-three historic properties ranging from the mountains to the coast. Special attractions like Tryon Palace in New Bern operate with a combination of state appropriations and private endowment funds. The beauty of Old Salem in Winston-Salem is made possible largely by private funds, but the state has long recognized the value of the site to its citizens and for years has made a large appropriation available to Old Salem on a regular basis. Scores of other historic properties in North Carolina also receive occasional assistance from the state or federal government in the form of grants.

While the Division of Archives and History has been directly involved with historic preservation at least from the time of its efforts to save Fort Raleigh in the early 1930s, the state also has been well-served by a strong nonprofit organization devoted to saving and enhancing important structures and sites. With the formation of the Society for the Preservation of Antiquities in 1939 (later the Historic Preservation Society of North Carolina), Tar Heels forged an organization that would educate many citizens to the importance of preservation.

In 1975, Tar Heel preservationists again developed an innovative organization when they formed the Historic Preservation Fund of North Carolina. This unique body was the first of its kind in the nation. Its purpose was to save historically valuable structures by devising marketing and funding strategies outside traditional methods. To date, the Fund has saved scores of historic properties in North Carolina, usually by sale to private individuals. Recognizing their complementary natures, the Fund and the Preservation Society merged at the start of 1984 to become the Historic Preservation Foundation of

North Carolina. With the newly acquired strength gained from such unity, the Foundation promises not only to build upon the success of its parents but to be even stronger in its youthful vigor than they were in their maturity.

The future of historic preservation in North Carolina seems bright. Despite decreasing levels of funding for preservation by the federal government, state and local governments continue to be generous in their support of Tar Heel history. As the pressures to conserve existing resources increase, developers and others realize the importance of historic preservation and are attracted to many of the tax incentives it offers.

Anyone who visits North Carolina cities like Charlotte, New Bern, Durham, Asheville, Tarboro and Salisbury sees startling evidence of the vital role that historic preservation can play in commercial and residential development. The keen interest of local preservationists in many Tar Heel communities promises that historic preservation will be a prominent feature of North Carolina for years to come. For if historic preservation succeeds, it succeeds best and most completely at the local level.

Tar Heels have a proud past. Their continuing commitment to the preservation and utilization of historic properties is one of the clearest manifestations of their pride in the past.

A native Tar Heel, Price has been director of the Division of Archives and History and state historic preservation officer since 1981. He is the author/editor of a number of publications, most recently serving as consulting editor of the five-volume series, *The Way We Lived in North Carolina.*

David M. "Carbine" Williams seemed most at home in his workshop, now in the permanent collection of the Museum of History. "I didn't want the Feds to get it," he told Governor Robert W. Scott when he donated his collection of guns.

Sensitive to the contributions of the past, North Carolinians have preserved sites of important endeavors, including Chowan County Courthouse, built in 1767, and the Asheville home of the state's most famous novelist, Thomas Wolfe.

Courtesy NCDA&H

Courtesy NCDA&H

43

The experiences and skills of the past, though rare, are still practiced today in North Carolina. For a taste of pioneer life, hardy folks have retraced Daniel Boone's original mountain route. They were led for many years by Chief Scout of the wagon train Ivey Moore.

Survival often meant fashioning what was needed from available resources. But creating something of beauty that also gave pleasure required a special talent that only a few possessed. That talent still exists today.

Good Ole Boys and Gentlemen

BY LAWRENCE MADDRY

Many times, since moving to the Old Dominion, I have been asked — as a Tar Heel born and bred — to explain the difference between a North Carolinian and a Virginian.

I think the answer is found in the way each regards a tree.

The Virginian, when asked to form a mental picture of a tree, invariably fills his mind with a family tree. He envisions a towering oak, a noble specimen with either an aristocrat or patriot twirling on every stem.

Ask a Carolinian to think of a tree, and he dreams of something entirely different. He sees a small tree. But there is a very big possum in it!

The difference is that the Virginian is reflective. The Carolinian is practical. How many Virginians does it take to change a light bulb? The answer is four. One to change the bulb; three to sit around and reflect on how great the old bulb was.

By contrast, it takes only two Carolinians to change a light bulb. One to change the bulb, another to fetch the barbecue sandwiches.

It is not that North Carolina does not have plenty of history to reflect upon. North Carolinians were conducting meetings, holding church services and producing offspring on Roanoke Island—Virginia Dare, for instance— more than 20 years before Jamestown. "But they disappeared. It didn't count. The country started in the Old Dominion," the Virginian replies. By that logic, civilization began not with Adam but after Noah.

Yet, convoluted logic is the essence of Virginia thinking. Let me give you an example. I once compared the crabs of the respective states. The Virginia crab seemed to me, after long observation, to be tentative and tended to go around in circles when approaching its prey. The Carolina crab seemed much more logical. It went straight for what it wanted without hesitation. In short, it seemed more direct.

After publishing my findings on the subject, noting that the Virginia crab seemed to go about in circles, I received a letter from a Norfolk lady.

"Yes," she wrote, "but our crabs go around in the very best circles." Only a Virginian could have written such a letter.

Indeed that was the attitude of Col. William Byrd, one of the first Virginians to set foot in North Carolina. In his "Histories of the Dividing Line Betwixt Virginia and North Carolina," written in the 1720s, he badmouthed Tar Heels for consuming so much pork that they spoke with a grunt. He found the Carolinians to be dirty, unaffected and, well, not Virginians. Beautiful.

What he really discovered, without knowing it, was the good ole boy. Tom Wolfe, the very good writer from Virginia, not the immortal Tom Wolfe from Asheville, once explained the good ole boy:

"It usually means he has a good sense of humor and enjoys ironic jokes, is tolerant and easygoing enough to get along in long conversations at places like on the corner and has a reasonable amount of physical courage."

North Carolina is a state of good ole boys. Zeb Vance was one. The late Gov. W. Kerr Scott was certainly one. Jim Graham, the Secretary of Agriculture, is another. Ditto "Catfish" Hunter, the former Yankee pitcher, and New York Timesman Tom Wicker. James Taylor is a good ole boy, too. But more so when he sings "I'm a Steam-Roller, Baby" than the tender ballad, "Carolina On My Mind."

Having a good sense of humor and enjoying ironic jokes is the essence of the Tar Heel. Where in Virginia would one find the kicking machine that Tom Haywood constructed down in Craven County?

You know the one I'm talking about. It was built to allow a man to kick himself in the seat by setting a series of brogans in motion. And who in Virginia would organize a "Man Will Never Fly Society," such as the one that meets each year near Kill Devil Hills? "Birds Fly; Men Drink" is their motto. They argue that two Wrights made a wrong at Kitty Hawk.

Then what is the Virginian? I dunno. He wants us to think of him as a gentleman. That is the phrase—"a Virginia gentleman." No people on earth spend more time arguing about what a gentleman is than Virginians. They have even named a bourbon for the phrase. In truth, far too much time is spent on the subject in Virginia than is seemly.

As Robert Smith Surtees once wrote: "The only infallible rule we know is that the man who is always talking about being a gentleman never is one."

Perhaps I have been too hard on my neighbors here to the north. The two states are good friends. Virginia is a noble place. And history books tell us Virginia is the mother of Presidents.

They neglect to say who the father was. A Carolinian, no doubt.

Maddry is a columnist for the Virginian-Pilot in Norfolk, Va. which also serves residents of north eastern North Carolina. His Carolina roots go back to Laurinburg and Chapel Hill where he attended The University of North Carolina at Chapel Hill. A Korean War veteran, Maddry also worked for The Raleigh Times in the sixties.

The Thrill of College Sports

BY CLARENCE "BIG HOUSE" GAINES

In the 40 years of my career as a coach and athletic director, I have experienced a lot of thrills in sports. I've seen thousands of youngsters come of age, as they competed on the playing field.

I've seen people like Earl Monroe, who helped Winston-Salem State University win the NCAA College Division Basketball Championship in 1967 and then went on to a first-round draft choice in the National Basketball Association, playing with the Baltimore Bullets and later the New York Knicks.

Cleo Hill was another first-round draft choice in 1961.

It also was a thrill in 1953 to win the CIAA basketball championship just four years after we started recruiting basketball players.

In the 1950's, it was a thrill to watch track star Elias Gilbert, under Wilbur Ross' coaching, win the NAIA Championship in hurdling.

Much has been accomplished in North Carolina sports during the past 40 years.

John McLendon, who was the "father of black basketball," taught us all a lot in his own way. He embarrassed a lot of us with his fine teams at North Carolina College (now North Carolina Central University) in Durham. But he raised the quality level of basketball in the conference.

Beyond that, a most pervasive accomplishment was the role that college sports played in integration.

It was during that crucial time in the late 1950's and early 1960's that racial barriers began to fall, and star athletes like David Thompson at N.C. State University, Mike Malloy at Davidson, and Phil Ford at the University of North Carolina at Chapel Hill, perhaps unknowingly, played a major role in what happened.

It was a time when sports emerged as a rallying point for communities and for fans all over the state. People got together to cheer for their team. It didn't matter whether players were black or white. It was "the team" that was important.

This attitude and phenomenon carried over into other aspects of life across the state as well. Sports now have become a great social force. Just check the parking lots outside football stadiums across the state on Saturday afternoons to see all the tailgate parties.

North Carolina, Winston-Salem specifically, was the site of one of the first

integrated college basketball games in the South.

It was a situation developed by Dr. James Hamilton, athletic director at High Point College, and the Athletic Department at Winston-Salem State University.

We had paid to bring in the NAIA champions for several years to play a two-day tournament with High Point College and WSSU. Dr. Hamilton suggested, "Why don't we just play each other?"

And so it was in the early 1960's that two small colleges, just 17 miles apart, met on the basketball court.

These are the milestones that stand out in my mind about college sports in North Carolina's history.

Certainly moments of induction into sports halls of fame on six occasions are memorable also. Seeing a building bearing one's name etches an indelible memory.

But in the end the greatest satisfaction, the greatest thrill, I have had as a part of sports is traveling around the country seeing people, many who had been "written off" by some as not likely to achieve any success in life, who have gone on from their college sports careers to become responsible citizens contributing to society.

Almost everywhere I go across the country I meet an athlete who has been part of my life. He is now pulling someone's tooth or defending someone in court. It is these times and these people who, to me, are the great thrills of sport.

He's won more basketball games than any active college coach in America. Gaines has been head coach at Winston-Salem State University since 1947 and collected title after title from the Central Intracollegiate Athletic Association. A Kentucky native, he is a graduate of Morgan State in Baltimore, Md., and holds a Master's from Columbia University.

"The Spitter" Comes Home

BY GAYLORD PERRY

As you browse through the rosters of professional sports teams past and present, they are generously sprinkled with the names of people from North Carolina. It shows vividly that the Tar Heel state has been a big contributor to the pool of sports talent in the country.

The names strike a familiar chord immediately. Charlie "Choo Choo" Justice, Enos "Country" Slaughter, Sonny Jergensen, Roman Gabriel, Smokey Burgess, David Thompson, Phil Ford, Sam Jones, Mike Cardwell, Tommy Helms, Tony Cloninger. The list is too long to recount here but the North Carolina hometowns of these figures span the length and breadth of the state including small town, large cities and even some country crossroads.

Some of this talent was discovered almost by accident.

The story is told that a semi-professional baseball team was playing baseball in a pasture near the Greene County town of Hookerton and a baseball scout noticed the game as he was driving by. What really got his attention was one of the players who was not wearing shoes. When he came to bat, he hit the ball so hard that the scout was surprised, so he took a closer look.

He signed up that shoeless player and he went on to star with the San Francisco Giants in the 1960's. His name was Jim Ray Hart.

I'm sure there are many other similar stories that have emerged from the sandlots and playgrounds around the state. It's a good sign that the state continues to see its citizens go on to a higher level of professional sports.

I usually talk more about baseball than other sports because I am more closely tied to that sport. Since I have retired from the game, I have the opportunity to look more closely at the youngsters who will some day be the stars of the big leagues.

Baseball can play a very beneficial role in a youngster's development. It's great to see little leaguers jell into a team that goes on to a championship. The team gives them something to strive for individually and collectively and when they reach their goal, it's gratifying.

Baseball has brought parents and children closer together. It's easier to get parents to the ball park than it is to the PTA. They can all participate whether as a player, coach or fan. And they have.

Minor league baseball in North Carolina has had a colorful history. Back in the 1940's and 1950's, almost any town that had anything resembling a baseball park had a minor league baseball team. And the games brought out the townsfolk religiously.

Later, the minor league system changed and many of those teams faded away. But today, minor league baseball is bouncing back. There's not as many teams as there were at one time, but the baseball that's being played must be entertaining the fans because they keep coming back.

It is the sand lots, playgrounds and the minor league parks where the big leaguers grow up. So many have grown up in North Carolina and more will grow up here in the future.

It could be said that baseball has been good for North Carolina. But it also would follow that North Carolina has been good for baseball.

A star pitcher for a number of major league baseball teams, Gaylord Perry won the Cy Young award in both the American and National Leagues. He was a member of five All-Star teams. Now a farmer in Williamston, N.C., Perry is the author of "Me and the Spitter: An Autobiographical Confession."

"The Holy Grub" — Eastern Style

BY DENNIS ROGERS

It is not easy being the world's foremost expert on the "Holy Grub." The person so annointed must be diligent in his research, steadfast in his opinions and devoted to his calling. It is a job fraught with perils, not the least of which is being tolerant in the face of fools.

Goodness knows I have tried. I have sat patiently gripping the cold neck of a Pepsi bottle until my knuckles turn white while others rattle on endlessly about the virtues of roasted hog meat they claim is barbecue. Forgive them, pig cookers, for they know not what they say.

The problem seems to be that some people think barbecue is nothing more than selected cuts of dead pig flesh cooked and eaten. They fail to see it as the cultural, social and, dare I say it, almost religious experience it is.

For those who would join the True Believers in our sacred mission to enlighten the world, I offer the following guide to pigging out in true Eastern North Carolina fashion. While it would be easier to explain the innards of a neutron bomb or why the Mona Lisa grins, I will be glad to do what I can.

First of all, would-be barbecue cooks must move to North Carolina. Air quality makes it impossible to cook the "Holy Grub" outside the confines of our beloved Tar Heelia. In fact, few people know that former President Jimmy Carter, who has family in North Carolina, issued an executive order banning the cooking of barbecue outside of North Carolina. But he'd probably deny it.

And you can't live just anywhere in North Carolina. Resist the siren song of those who would shout grand and glorious tales of heavenly pigs in Western North Carolina. Do not listen when they sidle up to you and mutter words like "Shelby" or "Lexington" in your hungry ears. Be strong and come East.

Imagine a football. Place one tip of your football in Raleigh. Place the other tip in New Bern. Then outline your football to include Enfield to the North and Pink Hill to the South. That is where you must live to enjoy a steady and necessary diet of good pig.

After you have been there for several years — no one ever claimed this was easy — or better yet, after several generations, buy yourself a hat that advertises farm products, preferably some herbicide that no one has ever heard of. How you curl the bill is a matter of personal preference, one of the few permitted.

Get a wooden drink crate, the kind with 24 little cubbyholes, and learn to sit, lean back and spit without leaving evidence on your shirt or falling backwards on your butt.

Learn to pour peanuts into a Pepsi bottle without spilling a single one.

Master the art of keeping a cigarette in one side of your mouth and a toothpick in the other until you can invariably reach for the right one without hesitation. Burning toothpicks taste awful and make you look silly.

Love your Mama, Hank Williams, Jr., stock car racing, stewed okra and tomatoes and the joy of a good dog, preferably one that can ride in the back of a pickup without staggering.

Marry a woman with two first names. Some suggestions are Mary Lou, Betty Jean and Jeannie Lynn. Muffy is not acceptable.

Learn to live on cold pork and beans, Vienna sausage, liver pudding and crackers

during hunting season. Hunting seasons, shall we say, are often matters of personal choice in these parts.

You must go to church, dislike all politicians except the ones who do you personal favors, loathe Charlotte, know how to light a cigarette with a book of matches using only one hand even though the truck window is open — you do have a truck, don't you? — and know the first names of all of your grandfather's brothers and sisters and who they married. Why they married them is never discussed in public.

And when you can check the head on a jar of stumphole whiskey and when you can repair a pickup truck using nothing but bailing wire and electrician's tape and when you can open a Pepsi on a nailhead and when you can plow straight without looking back and when you can wear white socks and tell 'em all where to go, then you can cook barbecue.

And not before.

Oh, did I forget something?

How do you cook it?

That's simple.

Kill a hog, put that sucker over some fire, cook it until it is done, put some stuff on it and eat it.

Shucks, that's the easy part.

The raconteur of eastern North Carolina, Rogers has published three collections of his popular columns, which have appeared in the News and Observer since 1976. A native of Wilson, he cut his writing teeth at newspaper stints in Chapel Hill, Fayetteville and Charlotte. In non-writing moments, he's likely to be seen on the stage, acting.

Barbecue Western Style

BY JAMES E. LAMBETH, JR.

Down East in North Carolina the folks speak in glowing terms about THEIR barbecue and how THEY have the secret potion for the finest barbecue ever tasted on this planet.

However, the Down East folks share that misconception because they have not partaken of the REAL barbecue. That happens to be the product of North Carolina's piedmont area.

Many go even farther to specify that Davidson County is the home of REAL barbecue.

It is a dish which has satisfied the palates of prince and pauper alike, cuisine that each can equally appreciate for its many fine qualities and proper taste.

Western barbecue (that is piedmont North Carolina barbecue) is the finest there is. Theories about this fact are bountiful — almost as numerous as the stars in the skies — but many who know the intricacies of this delightful and delectable delicacy say western barbecue is the best because only pork shoulder is used to make it. That's different from the Down East barbecue which includes the whole hog. The "whole hog" barbecue naturally includes the bad with the good.

The more selective method of using only the shoulders means that only the "good" part of the hog is used to make REAL barbecue.

Another theory is that the sauce used in making western barbecue is better than that used in other places where a somewhat reasonable facsimilie of barbecue is served. The sauce of the west tends to be spicier and brings out the full flavor of each morsel.

It is not suggested that anyone attempt to obtain the recipes for any of the sauces, however. Those are well-kept secrets, as closely guarded almost as the gold in Fort Knox.

Quite often when those who hold those intimate secrets are asked about sauce ingredients they choose to quickly begin talking about the weather, their Uncle George or simply leave the room to avoid making some inhospitable comment to such a rude intrusion.

Still another reason why western barbecue is best comes from the fact that it is cooked over hickory coals. That differs again from the Down East variety where the source of heat is often electricity. The hickory coals give additional flavor to the succulent meat. I don't know of any odor or quality that electricity can impart to anything quite the way hickory embers do.

But enough for theories. The fact simply is that western barbecue is a connoisseur's delight. People love it any way it is served. And word has spread about this diner's delight to places like New York City and Atlanta. Even the best kept secrets eventually are disclosed and the world finds out.

The origins of REAL barbecue go back more than a hundred years in piedmont North Carolina, although some theorize that it may all have started with the cave man when lightning may have struck a hickory tree where either some venison or boar was hanging to cure. The ensuing fire roasted the meat to such fine quality that barbecuing became a way of life even then.

So today it is that barbecue is held in such high esteem that those who say they don't like it comprise such small numbers that a convention of those misguided souls would leave room in a street corner telephone booth.

It is favored food of Tar Heel politicians for they eat it continuously along the campaign trail. And the concensus seems to be that western barbecue is more satisfying. A formal

vote on the matter would show the same results.

And no self-respecting barbecue officianado would think of having this hallowed food without hushpuppies, small balls of cornmeal dough deep fried to a goldren brown and served piping hot alongside the barbecue.

The hushpuppy is said to have been derived quite by accident when a piece of dough was dropped into some hot grease and when it was retrieved was tossed to some barking dogs, who immediately ceased their barking.

Little did the cooks know what they would start for later generations to enjoy — along with REAL barbecue.

Though presidents and kings, princes and politicians and just plain folks have soothed their hunger with this succulent repast, legions still debate its merits from place to place.

Barbecue has even been the topic of debate in North Carolina's legislative chambers where Lexington, N.C., was designated as the "Hickory-Cooked Barbecue Capital of Piedmont North Carolina."

It was the feeling of many that the designation should have made Lexington the "Hickory-Cooked Barbecue Capital of the World" but pressure from Down East would not allow the truth about REAL barbecue to be revealed in such a resolution.

The truth can be found, however, in any one of many barbecue restaurants in piedmont North Carolina.

Lambeth is a lifelong resident of Davidson County. A three-term member of the N.C. House of Representatives, he is chairman of the Wildlife Resources Committee. Chairman of the board of Lambeth Limited, he is a past director of Rotary International and a life-long connoisseur of barbecue.

Return to the New River Valley

BY GLENN MORRIS

The roads mostly go where the river doesn't — from one near-flat space to the next near-flat space. Occasionally, the roads follow the banks of the New River, bordering what little narrow bottom land there is. Such flats, perhaps the richest, most fertile ground in Ashe and Alleghany counties, embroider the river in a helter-skelter pattern. The flats occur sporadically; their location is unpredictable. You discover them along one bank, but coil around a crook in the river and they jump to the other side.. That's when your riverside road corkscrews away from the flow, threading between the seemingly countless hills of the New River's headwater country.

Where there is level land, there is a farm, or a store, or a community. The farms require only enough flat land for a house and barn, and perhaps a field for silage. And since the best farmable land was acquired generations ago, there is not much left for newcomers. Twisting this observation slightly, there are not many people willing to live on a tilt, so the populations of these two counties increase but slowly. This single reason—that there is not enough land left for those who might wish to live near the New River headwaters—is probably why things never seem to change. The homesteads you see are the homesteads you might have seen if you visited two generations ago.

Why? Perhaps it's because the native sons and daughters of the New River country won't live anywhere else. They leave home for school—maybe—and inevitably return. Those who don't leave figure there is not much they need beyond the valley. They've got a roof, food, friends and the river, which gave, directly or indirectly, everything else to them—especially the land.

There is no land like it anywhere else in the state—so curvy and undulating that the most memorable stretches of state road are those on which it is safe enough to pass a pickup truck ferrying a heifer from one patch of emerald sod to another. There is an unwritten rule of right-of-way on these farm-to-market roads: tractors first, then combines, then school buses, then RFDs and, finally, pickups. Anybody else who thinks they have to hurry here learns patience. You don't hurry, you amble. You cruise, inching your way into Sparta or Jefferson with the speed of a wooley-bear caterpillar rumpling for shelter.

North Carolina native Glenn Morris is a graduate of Princeton University. He spent five and one-half years as Landscape Editor and Outdoor Living Editor of *Southern Living* and is currently working on his own first book with UNC Press. Over the past 16 years, Morris has been a regular visitor to the New River country in Alleghany County.

You measure the height of neighbor's corn and count his calves along the way, or spot a downed fence and a scurrying groundhog. Hurrying to town or home won't milk the cows any faster, nor will it make the corn grow taller quicker or speed up the canning of summer's harvest. What is unfinished today is tomorrow's starting task. In New River country, you learn to chip away at time, not slash at it. After all, the river set the tempo long ago, and it is too old to hurry. But it is, if nothing else, deliberate.

Geologists say the New is very old and theorize that only the Nile basin has carried water longer. Its meandering path is serendipity—all the characteristics of a mature river, a lazy curvaceous wander and shallow depth. The peregrinations of the New River are one of its most vexing and endearing charms—you cross it when you least expect it. There is never a landmark sloping of the land before you view the languid coils; you simply round a bend in the road and it is there.

The New River is sweetly and simply inexorable. It chose a path and stuck to it. When cataclysmic upheavals raised the earth below it, it simply accelerated its flow and cut into the rock faster than the rock could rise; hence, a great curiosity about the river: It is older than the hills and mountains through which if flows.

In other words, the New River is responsible for almost everything in North Carolina's northwest corner. Where it left flats, men built homes and towns; where the flood plain widened and settled rich alluvial deposits, farmers sowed corn and squeezed tractor-wide roads beside the fields; where the river, already shallow, is fordable, they crossed or poled flat-bottomed boats. They also fished and generations swung free from a rope-tasseled tree to plunge into its icy purity or fought the icy flows that accumulated on this gentle grey matriarch each winter.

Valley residents have known all the joy and anger this river of life has given them— the crushing, bone-chilling cold; the chill-slop of spring's muddy fields; the searing summer days that yield to morning dews; and autumn's color rampage above the dark waters. They've known it for all their lives. They've cherished the sequence of seasons and the river's changing moods—winter-still, spring-angry, summer-somnolent and autumn's rejuvenation. They even fought for the river. In a classic combine or computer battle, the tractor force defeated the megawatt bucks who sought to flood more than 40,000 acres of New River bottom land, and they won—for both the river and their way of life. In 1976, Congress declared 21.5 miles of the New River wild and scenic, which was made law-of-the-land with then-President Ford's signature.

The residents of the valley didn't need Congress to tell them the New River is wild and scenic. They already knew, just as their great-grandfathers did.

In 1980, Robert Gambill "geed" when he should have "hawed" as our canoe entered Duck Roose Rapids. The river swallowed the mistake with glee and laundered the two of us and our canoe onto a sandy spit. That was my first dealing in the river, though its countryside had served as a respite for more than 15 years.

I would plunge again in another time and place—daydreaming to starboard when I should have paddled for port. The river washed me free of my errant concentration, again. But without ever stepping or plunging into it, I have been able to draw deeply from the New a satisfaction and understanding of time. It must be bittersweet to live on the river, for it can take as rapidly and unpredictably as it gives. But to visit there reminds me of how temporary many worries are.

To see the river again is to learn the meaning of proportion. Yes, things have changed along the New River—but how much? How significant is the change to a life of the hundreds of millions of years that the river already has recorded? Each time I view it, it is steady, sometimes swollen and angry, but inevitably it returns to a serene equilibrium that whittles its place more definitely into the upstart hills that men for generations have come to call home.

It is a home and way of life they share. And much of the credit belongs to the New, which carried away—particle by particle— every bit of land which was *not* an ideal place to live, raise a family and till the soil.

The
North Carolina
Illustrated Timeline

CHAPTER 3

INTRODUCTION TO THE TIMELINE

The North Carolina Illustrated Timeline is intended to provide a connected, developmental outline of the significant and molding events in the rich, 400-year history of the Tar Heel state. The Timeline—is outlined, arranged in chronological order, color coded by era, illustrated and indexed on page 174.

The illustrations were selected with a view toward emphasizing the personal side of history and linking people to events. It has been in the daily lives of the small as well as the great that North Carolina has emerged as a leading state in the South and an increasingly consequential state in the nation. Something of the quality of the state as a whole is lodged in the mind and heart of each of us. We trust that the North Carolina Illustrated Timeline bears witness to the humanistic in history and places our state's past in unique perspective.

Discovery and Exploration: 1524-1662.

Spanish, French and English explorers visited what is now North Carolina. After several unsuccessful efforts to found a colony here, a trickle of permanent settlers began moving south from Virginia in the mid-1600s.

Spanish Carolina: 1524-1588.
French and Spanish explorers made contact with the Indians of coastal North Carolina and trekked as far inland as the Appalachians in search of precious metals, a sea-route to the Pacific or a shortcut to the mines of Mexico.

Raleigh's Roanoke Colonies: 1567-1590.
Sir Walter Raleigh obtained from Queen Elizabeth I the right to establish a colony on Roanoke Island. Both of his efforts failed, his second colony disappearing after reaching the island.

The South Part of Virginia—and Carolana: 1607-1650.
Settlers at Jamestown tried in vain after 1607 to find Raleigh's Lost Colony. Meanwhile, several projects to spread settlements south to "Carolana" were unsuccessful.

The First Permanent Settlers: 1653-1662.
By 1655, although New England Puritans gave up after an attempt to colonize the Cape Fear River area, the first Virginians had established themselves in Carolana around the Albemarle Sound region.

Proprietary North Carolina: 1663-1729.

King Charles II in 1663 granted what are now North and South Carolina to eight powerful noblemen known as the Lords Proprietors. North Carolina developed slowly until the Crown resumed control of the colony in 1729.

Laying the Foundations: 1663-1672.
Despite frustrations of bad weather and other problems, the Carolina colony struggled into existence, though the policies of the Proprietors were not always popular with the settlers.

The Albemarle Rebellion: 1673-1689.
Colonists waged fierce political (and sometimes military) combat with each other over land, tax and other issues. Proprietary authority carried little weight in the settlement of these issues.

The Quaker Epoch: 1691-1706.
For two decades, the leading political and religious force was the Quaker sect. John Archdale, a Quaker governor, helped entrench Quaker power in the colony.

The Cary Rebellion: 1704-1711.
After a struggle against the rising power of the Anglicans, the power of the Quakers was broken by armed overthrow.

Of Pirates and Indians: 1710-1718.
Blackbeard and other pirates haunted the North Carolina coast while Indians obstructed expansion inland. Help from Virginia and South Carolina colonists destroyed the strength of both Indians and pirates by 1718.

The Close of the Proprietary: 1713-1729.
By the 1720s, North Carolina was beginning to grow more rapidly, its first towns starting to emerge. In 1729, the English Crown took over direct rule of the colony.

The Royal Colony: 1730-1776.

North Carolina prospered under Royal control but shared colonial resentment over certain British policies and joined in resistance to those policies.

A Sea of Troubles: 1730-1761.
Progress was accompanied by internal political conflict and the external menace of enemies to the colonists.

Elements of Style: 1749-1768.
The rise of churches, printing presses, towns and Masonic lodges were among the evidences of growing enlightenment in Royal North Carolina.

Regulators and Sons of Liberty: 1765-1771
Sectional differences led to the War of Regulation, and troubles with England mounted to a crisis by 1776.

The Coming of the Revolution: 1773-1776.
Protests over taxation and other Royal policies led to a movement for independence and the onset of fighting in North Carolina between Redcoats and Patriots.

The Revolutionary Epoch: 1776-1800.

Tar Heels helped win American independence and begin a new nation under a Federal Constitution.

The War for Independence: 1776-1783.
Though severely tried in battles at home and on the seas, North Carolinians did their part in defeating British military power.

North Carolina and the Nation: 1784-1800.
North Carolinians submitted only reluctantly to the federal system but made continued progress in the early years of statehood within the new nation.

Timeline Author

Thomas C. Parramore, a native of Winton, North Carolina, earned his Ph.D. in history from the University of North Carolina. A foremost authority on the history of his home state, he is the author of eight books on the subject, the most recent of which, *North Carolina: The History of an American State*, published in 1983, is currently being used as the history textbook in the public schools. He also has authored numerous articles and presented a great many papers on different aspects of North Carolina history. Listed among the *Who's Who in International Education*, Dr. Parramore has been an Associate Professor of History at Meredith College since 1978.

The Age of the Antifederalists: 1800-1833.

Under the rule of antifederalist policies, North Carolina slumbered through the opening decades of the 19th century—an era of public apathy and slow economic and cultural gains.

The Jeffersonian Years: 1800-1812.
The Republican era under Thomas Jefferson ushered in a swing away from a strong federal government, and public expenses and taxes were kept low. The state government became unresponsive to the needs of the people, however, and dissatisfaction with social and economic conditions prevailed.

The Rip Van Winkle Years—
North Carolina Asleep: 1813-1833.
A new war with England, emigration of Tar Heels to the southwest and other difficulties contributed to the bleakness of the early decades of the century.

The Great Awakening: 1829-1862.

A new political party, the Whigs, roared into existence in the 1830s and waged a strong campaign for internal improvements and educational progress. In the next quarter-century, North Carolina knew the greatest reform movement in its history.

Old Rip Begins to Stir: 1829-1839.
Reform of the state constitution and a surge of railroad construction marked the early phase of the new era.

The Reform Era: 1840-1862.
A free-school system and other socio-economic improvements sponsored by the Whigs were followed by further gains under the rejuvenated Democrats.

Civil War and Reconstruction: 1861-1877.

Slavery and the States Rights issue brought a devastating civil war and defeat to the South. Postwar Reconstruction, though bringing freedom for blacks, found North Carolina humiliated and licking its wounds.

The War in North Carolina: 1861-1865.
Northern forces invaded the Tar Heel coast and ravaged the eastern and western counties throughout most of the war.

The Death and Revival
of Conservative Rule: 1865-1874.
Black emancipation and temporary disenfranchisement for many whites brought constitutional reform in North Carolina. The return of conservative rule, however, curtailed the course of social revolution.

Good Times and Bad: 1865-1938.

Fueled by industrial growth, North Carolina finally began to enjoy renewed economic development, but the rise of Jim Crow laws limited the gains primarily to white people.

Industrial and Economic Progress: 1865-1892.
Tobacco, furniture and textiles were the leading industries in North Carolina's industrial surge.

The "Red-Shirt" Years: 1894-1901.
Laws restricting the rights of black people culminated with the virtual disenfranchisement of blacks.

The Progressive Era: 1901-1915.
North Carolina joined enthusiastically in the Progressive reform period sweeping the nation.

World War I: 1916-1919.
Many Tar Heels saw service in Europe during the war, which came as close as the coastal waters of North Carolina.

The 1920s: 1920-1929.
With the war over, Tar Heels and other Americans lost interest in reform and entered a decade of more material pursuits. But many North Carolinians failed to benefit from the new wealth.

The Great Depression: 1929-1938.
The Depression plunged North Carolina into economic crisis. The Roosevelt "New Deal" relieved much of the suffering but did not end the basic economic woes of both the state and the nation.

The Modern Era: 1940-1984.

World War II cost many lives but gave North Carolina and America the economic boost to end the Depression and create vast opportunities for growth and prosperity. There also was a new focus on civil rights and human equality.

World War II Era: 1940-1946.
Many North Carolinians fought on foreign soil. Military bases and shipbuilding were among the economic benefits brought to the state.

Gains and Losses: 1948-1958.
Outdoor dramas, a state art museum and the new Research Triangle were only a few consequences of the prosperous postwar period.

Civil Rights and Wrongs: 1954-1969.
Pushed by federal initiative, a new era of minority liberation dawned as the civil rights movement gained momentum.

And Just the Other Day... : 1971-1984.
Tar Heels entered a more conservative era in which industrialization, politics, conservation of natural resources, education and athletics were among their major concerns. They also committed themselves to the memorialization of the achievements of former times.

Spanish
Carolina

March 21, 1524

July 1526

May 1540

1558

August 24, 1566

March 21, 1524
Spanish adventurer
**Giovanni da
Verrazano,** sailing for
the French government,
was the first recorded
European to reach the
shores of what later
became North Carolina.
Looking across the
Outer Banks, he
thought Pamlico Sound
was the Pacific Ocean.

Courtesy NCDA&H

Courtesy NCDA&H

**July 1526
Luis Vazquez de
Ayllon** brought more
than 500 Spanish
settlers from the West
Indies to the lower Cape
Fear River to try to start
a colony. Unable to find
suitable land, they
moved to the South
Carolina coast where
they encountered a host
of problems, including
disease, hunger and bad
weather. After Ayllon
himself died, the 150
survivors returned in
the winter to the West
Indies.

May 1540
Spanish explorers under
Hernando de Soto,
marching north on foot
from the Gulf Coast of
Florida, traveled
through the south-
western mountains of
North Carolina in
search of gold and
probably reached the
present-day Asheville
area.

1558
Shipwrecked sailors,
thought to have been
from a Spanish ship,
were rescued by Indians
on the **Pamlico River.**
The sailors fashioned a
boat from canoes and,
using their shirts for a
sail, headed south
toward Spanish Florida.

August 24, 1566
Spaniards looking for
the **Chesapeake Bay**
landed briefly on the
coast of present
Currituck County. Led
by Pedro de Coronas,
they explored for a few
days but, encountering
no natives, gave up and
eventually returned to
the West Indies.

Courtesy NCDA&H

| 1567 | April 1567 | 1584 | July 13, 1584 | July 27, 1585 | June 18, 1586 |

1567
Under the reign of **Queen Elizabeth I,** England began to expand and challenge Spanish claims in the New World.

April 1567
Juan Pardo and other Spaniards from St. Helen's, an outpost on the South Carolina coast, explored some 350 miles inland to the North Carolina mountains in search of gold. They built and briefly occupied some small forts in the area where the first gold rush in the United States took place over 200 years later. These early Spaniards, however, found no gold.

1584
After obtaining permission from Queen Elizabeth I, **Walter Raleigh** dispatched two ships under Captains Phillip Amadas and Arthur Barlowe to the New World to find a good site for a colony.

Courtesy NCDA&H

July 13, 1584
Amadas and Barlowe landed on the Outer Banks of North Carolina at Cape Hatteras and laid claim to the land in the name of Queen Elizabeth.

July 27, 1585
Raleigh's first colonization expedition, a group of 108 men under the direction of Sir Richard Grenville, reached **Roanoke Island** and began the first English settlement in the New World. They built an earthen fort, which they named **Fort Raleigh,** and crude living quarters of wattle and bark. **Ralph Lane,** a soldier, had been appointed to govern this military colony, and artist John White was also a member of the expedition.

June 18, 1586
Lane's colonists, weary from hunger and fighting with local Indians, reluctantly abandoned Roanoke Island. They accepted a ride home to England with **Sir Francis Drake,** who had stopped by the island with his fleet on his return from an attack on the Spanish in the Caribbean. Only weeks later, Grenville returned from England with needed supplies and, finding the colony deserted, left 15 of his own men to hold the island for England before he sailed home.

Courtesy NCDA&H

63

July 22, 1587
Portuguese navigator **Simon Fernandez,** hired by Sir Walter Raleigh to transport a second colony to the New World to settle on the Chesapeake Bay, stopped at Roanoke Island to pick up Grenville's men. He put the colonists ashore there, however, and hurried off to attack a Spanish treasure fleet sailing west to the Azores. Although **John White,** the artist on Lane's expedition and the governor of this second colony, protested vigorously, he had no choice but to settle his 117 civilians, including 17 women and nine children, on the island.

Courtesy North Carolina Collection

August 13, 1587
Manteo, a Native American Indian who had been to England twice and returned to the New World with Gov. White and his people to serve as an interpreter, was baptized on Roanoke Island and dubbed "Lord of Roanoke" by the English.

August 18, 1587
Virginia, daughter of Eleanor and Ananias Dare and granddaughter of Gov. John White, was born on Roanoke Island. She was the first white child born in English America.

August 27, 1587
Gov. White was persuaded by the colonists to return to England to procure more supplies. The colonists already had decided to move about 50 miles inland, probably to the Albemarle Sound area, and make a new settlement where the Indians were friendlier and there was better farmland.

Courtesy NCDA&H

June 1588
A Spanish scouting vessel searched the south end of **Roanoke Island** for the English colonists. The Spaniards found clear signs of former habitation, but they did not encounter any people.

Courtesy NCDA&H

August 18, 1590	April 21, 1607	January 1608	October 29, 1618	February 1622

January 1608
A Virginia Indian chief led the first of several expeditions into north-eastern North Carolina in search of the **Lost Colonists.** Apparently, no traces were found of the missing Englishmen.

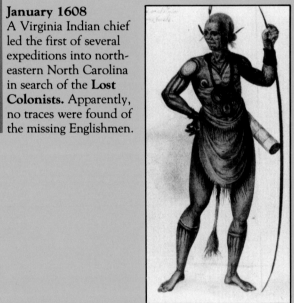

Courtesy North Carolina Collection

October 29, 1618
Sir Walter Raleigh was beheaded in England to appease the Spanish, against whom he had led raids in South America.

February 1622
John Pory, former Secretary of the Virginia colony, led explorers into the Chowan River area of North Carolina to investigate the potential of the region for English settlement.

August 18, 1590
On his granddaughter's third birthday, White, delayed by the Spanish Armada and open warfare between England and Spain on the high seas, finally was able to return to Roanoke Island. He found the colony deserted, and the only clue was the word "CROATOAN" carved on a tree. He tried to sail south to Croatoan (Hatteras) Island, hoping to find his people there, but a series of bad storms damaged his ship and forced his return to England instead. None of the people from this **"Lost Colony"** were ever heard from again.

April 21, 1607
The first **Jamestown** colonists reached the coast of Virginia. They established on the James River the first permanent English colony in America.

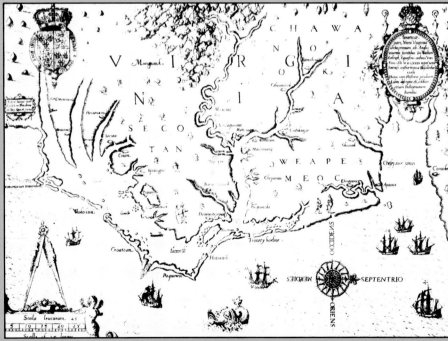

Courtesy NCDA&H

65

The First Permanent Settlers

October 30, 1629	August 29, 1650	September 1653	April 1654	Summer 1655	September 24, 1660

October 30, 1629
King Charles I granted all the land between Florida and Virginia and from ocean to ocean to his attorney general, **Sir Robert Heath.** This region then was known as "Carolana," in honor of the King. Three years later, after neither Englishmen nor French Huguenots would settle there, Heath assigned his rights to Sir Henry Maltravers. Maltravers also was unable ever to establish settlers there.

August 29, 1650
Explorers from Fort Henry (now Petersburg), Virginia, under **Edward Bland** entered North Carolina by land and visited the Tuscarora Indians of the Roanoke River, hoping to establish a fur trade with them.

September 1653
While visiting the Albemarle Sound region, fur trader **Nathaniel Batts** arranged the purchase of a large tract of Indian land for Francis Yeardley, a member of the Virginia legislature. The land is thought to have been on the north side of the sound, in the area around the mouths of the "three great rivers," in what is now Perquimans County.

April 1654
Francis Yeardley sent another party to the Albemarle to make plans for a settlement there. As agreed, he sent along a carpenter, Robert Bodnam, to build an English frame house for the Indian chief who had sold Yeardley the land, probably Chief Kiskatanewh of the Pasquotank tribe.

September 24, 1660
Batts bought a tract of land on the west side of the Pasquotank River from Yeopim Indians. This is the **oldest existing deed** for North Carolina property.

Courtesy NCDA&H

Summer 1655
Bodnam again went to the Albemarle, this time to build a house on the **Albemarle Sound** at the mouth of Salmon Creek for Batts to use as a fur-trading station. Batts probably used it seasonally before permanently moving to the Albemarle two or three years later. He may have been the first permanent English settler in North Carolina.

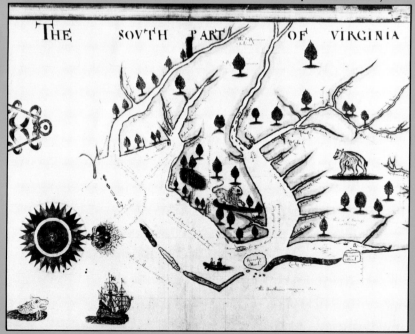

Courtesy NCDA&H

March 1, 1662

October 1662

March 24, 1663

May 1664

October 1664

Courtesy North Carolina Collection

March 1, 1662
Other Virginians followed Batts, and soon several families had settled in the Albemarle region, including Virginia farmer **George Durant,** who built a farmhouse on the east side of the Perquimans River. This point of land is still known as **Durant's Neck** in Perquimans County. Pictured above is a copy of the inscription from the Durant family Bible.

October 9, 1662
Because the number of settlers in the Albemarle had grown sufficiently, Gov. Berkeley of Virginia appointed **Samuel Stephens** "commander of the southern plantation," giving him authority over settlements on the Albemarle Sound.

October 1662
Disaffected **Puritans** from Massachusetts were said to have settled on the lower Cape Fear River. They seemed to have found the soil too thin and the Indians too thick, however, for all had left quite mysteriously by April 1663.

March 24, 1663
The old Heath-Maltravers grant having been annulled, a new charter for this vast tract of land, hereafter referred to as **"Carolina,"** was awarded by the new English monarch, King Charles II, to eight English noblemen who became known as the **Lords Proprietors.** The grant was a reward for the strong role these men had played in returning the English throne to the monarchy in 1660. They were given broad feudal governing powers, by which they had the authority to create government offices, make appointments, establish courts and collect taxes. The colonists were to be given the same rights as Englishmen.

Courtesy NCDA&H

May 1664
Puritans from Barbados and New England made another settlement on the **Cape Fear River.** They started a town (near present Brunswick) called **Charles Town,** and by 1666, about 800 people had settled over a stretch of some 60 miles of river country. Because of widespread dissatisfaction, however, they suddenly abandoned the area in 1667.

October 1664
William Drummond, a Scottish merchant from Virginia, was named the first proprietary governor of the newly formed coastal county known as Albemarle.

August 27, 1667

July 21, 1669

November 21, 1672

1673

October 1674

Courtesy Parramore Collection

October 1674
The Lords Proprietors mistakenly allowed the commissions of **Gov. John Jenkins,** himself a planter who opposed the Plantation Duty Act, and his council to expire. The Albemarle now had no legal government, although Jenkins continued to exercise the office of governor.

August 27, 1667
A terrible hurricane swept along the coast. After first ravaging the Cape Fear settlement, it moved northward and also destroyed most of the homes in the Albemarle region.

July 21, 1669
By a document known as the **Fundamental Constitutions,** possibly written by English philosopher John Locke (1632-1704), the Lords Proprietors wished to tighten their control on Carolina by changing to a feudal form of society and government. They believed this would enable them more easily to realize their proprietary aims of increased profits through large-scale expansion of trade in the Albemarle region. The plan was unrealistic, however, and never implemented.

November 21, 1672
George Fox, founder of the **Quakers,** visited the sparsely populated Albemarle region and, in the course of several weeks there, converted many of the settlers and planted the seeds for what eventually became a stronghold for the Quaker faith. Until the end of the 17th century, the Quakers were the only organized faith in the Albemarle settlements.

1673
England's **Plantation Duty Act** put a tax on tobacco not shipped directly to England. This angered some of the Albemarle planters who, because of shallow harbors, had to ship produce by small ships to Boston and other ports for transshipment.

Courtesy NCDA&H

Fall 1675	October 1676	July 15, 1677	December 1, 1677	December 16, 1677

December 16, 1677
On about this date, Miller was being tried at a Pasquotank River court for abuses of his office when word was received from Virginia that Eastchurch had arrived there and was raising an army to turn out the Jenkins people. The rebels raised forces to defend themselves, and civil war seemed likely. Eastchurch's untimely death, however, thwarted plans to invade the Albemarle and turn out the rebels.

December 1, 1677
A group of about 100 rebels opposing Miller, who strictly enforced the tax, armed themselves and, under the leadership of Jenkins and John Culpeper, launched **Culpeper's Rebellion.** They imprisoned Miller and once more seized control of the government.

Fall 1675
Surveyor-general and Speaker of the House of Burgesses **Thomas Eastchurch** and his supporters, opponents of Jenkins, seized control of the Albemarle government and jailed Gov. Jenkins. Eastchurch kept the title of Speaker but, in essence, became the governor of Albemarle County.

October 1676
With the Albemarle on the verge of civil war, Jenkins escaped from jail and recovered power from Eastchurch. Eastchurch then fled to England and received the endorsement of the Lords Proprietors, largely because he pledged total support of the Plantation Duty Act and the proprietary aims of expanding Albemarle's trade and territory.

July 15, 1677
Thomas Miller, Eastchurch's associate, reached the Albemarle to serve as acting governor while Eastchurch, unaware of the severity of the situation in Carolina, honeymooned for five months in the Caribbean with his new bride.

Photographed at right is the diorama reproduced by the North Carolina Department of Archives and History to represent **Culpeper's Rebellion.** The diorama depicts the waterfront along George Durant's plantation where Thomas Miller and several others were seized.

Courtesy NCDA&H

69

1678	Fall 1689	November 1691	August 17, 1695	December 9, 1696	November 1701

1678
The Lords Proprietors named one of themselves, **Seth Sothel,** to replace Jenkins, but Sothel was captured en route to America by Algerine pirates. He eventually was ransomed and finally arrived in the Albemarle about four years later.

Fall 1689
After nearly six years of Sothel's alleged abuse of power as governor, the spark of rebellion was rekindled among Albemarle's rebels who rose again and ousted him. The new governor, **Phillip Ludwell,** was a strong and fair leader who finally was able to impose peace and order on the distressed colony.

November 1691
The Lords Proprietors sent Ludwell to Charleston to serve as governor of the newly reorganized Carolina colony. Albemarle County ceased to exist, and Ludwell named planter **Thomas Jarvis** as deputy governor for the region north of the Cape Fear River, referred to for the first time as **"North" Carolina.**

August 17, 1695
Quaker **John Archdale,** a Lord Proprietor, took up duties in Charleston as the new governor of Carolina.

December 9, 1696
Bath County was created for colonists who had recently moved southward and settled around the lower Pamlico River.

November 1701
Henderson Walker, the Anglican deputy governor of the area north of Cape Fear, managed to get a law passed barring Quakers from holding public office. This set off a 10-year religious struggle in which the Quakers were sometimes in office and sometimes not.

Courtesy NCDA&H

Courtesy Guilford College Collection

December 15, 1701

1704

March 1705

March 8, 1706

Courtesy NCDA&H

December 15, 1701
An Anglican vestry, organized in Chowan Precinct, began building the colony's first Anglican chapel, **St. Paul's,** at what is now Edenton.

1704
Robert Daniel, deputy governor of North Carolina, invoked an English law requiring all public officials to take an oath of loyalty to the new English monarch, Queen Anne. Because of their religious beliefs against taking oaths, this again excluded Quakers from holding office, and all resigned.

Courtesy NCDA&H

March 21, 1705
After North Carolina Quakers petitioned against anti-Quaker policies, the Charleston administration appointed **Thomas Cary,** stepson of Quaker John Archdale, as the new deputy governor. Even though Cary was an Anglican, the Quakers thought they had won a victory.

March 27, 1705
Cary refused to change the policy on oaths, thereby proving that his sentiments were not with the Quakers after all.

March 8, 1706
As part of the growth and expansion attitude of the Lords Proprietors, the **Town of Bath** on the Pamlico River was laid out by **John Lawson.** It was incorporated and became the first town in North Carolina.

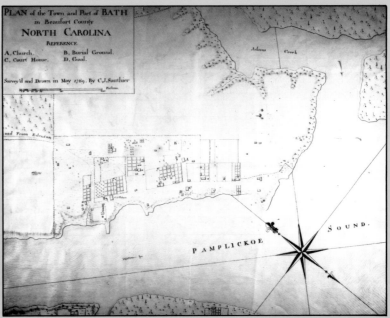

Courtesy NCDA&H

March 28, 1707 | October 12, 1708 | Summer 1710 | December 11, 1710 | January 1711

March 28, 1707
Quakers' complaints directly to the Lords Proprietors resulted in Cary being forced out and replaced by **William Glover,** believed to be a less stringent Anglican.

October 12, 1708
When technical deficiencies were found in Glover's appointment, the legislature reinstated Thomas Cary, who had now formed an **alliance with the Quakers,** as deputy governor. Anglicans and other Gloverites protested loudly, and civil war again seemed likely.

Courtesy NCDA&H

Summer 1710
As Carolina was beginning to attract other settlers from Europe, a Swiss land company headed by **Baron Christoph von Graffenried,** a leader of Swiss and German Protestants seeking religious freedom, settled about 500 people on 17,500 acres of land located at the junction of the Neuse and Trent rivers. The settlement was called **New Bern,** in honor of Bern, Switzerland, the former home of many of the settlers.

December 11, 1710
The Lords Proprietors, displeased and hoping to end conflict and confusion over the Anglican/Quaker quarrel, made North Carolina separate from South Carolina and named **Edward Hyde,** a cousin of Queen Anne, as the first governor of North Carolina.

Courtesy NCDA&H

January 1711
Hyde reached North Carolina, and his new Anglican government quickly set about recovering power from Cary and his Quaker allies. Cary came under constant persecution and was ordered to be arrested for various charges of wrong-doing. Rather than be taken captive, Cary and his followers launched a rebellion, mostly in **Bath County.** The Quakers supported him but, as pacifists, could not engage in armed action in his behalf.

June 30, 1711	Mid-September 1711	September 22, 1711	February 11, 1712	March 7, 1712	March 23, 1713

June 30, 1711
Cary's band attacked Hyde's headquarters on the Albemarle Sound. After a brief exchange of artillery and gunfire, Cary's forces were scattered, and the **Cary Rebellion** soon fell apart. Cary was arrested and sent to England for trial.

Mid-September 1711
While on a canoe expedition up the Neuse River, Baron Graffenried and Surveyor-general John Lawson (author of *A New Voyage to Carolina*) were captured by **Tuscarora Indians.** Lawson was accused of abuses of the Indians and executed a few days later. His death was a prelude to the Tuscarora War, the bloodiest Indian war ever fought on North Carolina soil.

September 22, 1711
The Tuscarora War opened as Catechna (now Contentnea) Creek Tuscaroras began attacking colonial settlements near New Bern and Bath Town. More than 130 whites were killed by war parties of Tuscarora, Neuse, Bear River, Machapunga and other Indian tribes. When the fighting continued over the next several months, a great many colonists began fleeing the colony, and public life nearly ceased to exist.

February 11, 1712
Responding to Gov. Hyde's desperate appeal for military assistance, South Carolina sent **Col. John Barnwell** and an army of approximately 500 Yamassee Indians, who reached Bath Town after marching through Tuscarora country. The Tuscarora War had come close to destroying the North Carolina colony by this time.

March 7, 1712
Barnwell's forces attacked the Tuscarora's **Fort Hancock** on Contentnea Creek (near present-day Grifton) and, after nearly a month of fighting, persuaded the Indians to agree to a truce and peace treaty. The fighting soon reopened, however, when Barnwell began selling off Indian prisoners as slaves.

March 23, 1713
Responding once again to Gov. Hyde's plea for assistance, South Carolina sent **Col. James Moore,** at the head of a large number of that colony's Indians, who attacked and destroyed **Fort Nohoroco** (also near Grifton), the Contentnea Creek stronghold of Chief Hancock. A great many Indians were killed which, in effect, ended the Indian war.

Courtesy NCDA&H

Courtesy NCDA&H

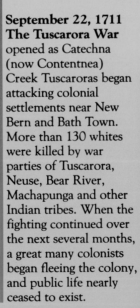

73

Early May 1713

October 2, 1713

September 1, 1715

June 1718

September 27, 1718

**Early May 1713
Chief Tom Blunt,** head of the neutral Tuscaroras of the Pamlico-Roanoke river region, signed a treaty with the North Carolina government promising aid against remaining enemy Indians. Most Tuscaroras, militant and neutral, eventually moved to New York. The defeat of the Tuscaroras opened up the heretofore unavailable but highly desirable interior regions of North Carolina to rapid expansion, thus becoming one of the major turning points in the history of the settlement of North Carolina.

**October 2, 1713
Beaufort,** North Carolina's third town, was laid off and named.

September 1, 1715
The first lots sold in a new town on Queen Anne's Creek in Chowan County. It was named **Edenton** in 1722 after Gov. Eden.

Courtesy NCDA&H

June 1718
Pirate partners **"Blackbeard"** and **Stede Bonnet** arrived at Topsail Inlet after plundering South Carolina shipping, then went their separate ways. Blackbeard won forgiveness from **Gov. Charles Eden,** settled at Bath Town and, for a time, became a privateer.

Courtesy Museum of Early Southern Decorative Arts, Winston-Salem

**September 27, 1718
Bonnet,** captured on the Cape Fear River by South Carolina militia, was taken to Charleston, where he was tried and hanged.

Courtesy NCDA&H

June 3, 1725
The first land-grants for lands on the **Cape Fear River** were issued, and many settlers rushed to take up valuable tracts there.

June 30, 1726
The first recorded lots were sold in the new town of **Brunswick** on the lower Cape Fear.

March 7, 1727
Virginia and North Carolina commissioners drove a stake in the ground on the banks of Currituck and began surveying the **dividing-line** between the two colonies. They completed the work in 1728. Pictured below is **Christopher Gale,** Chief Justice of North Carolina from 1712 to 1731, who served as one of the four commissioners from North Carolina.

Courtesy NCDA&H

November 22, 1718
Blackbeard, having renewed his piracy, was run down by Virginia forces at **Ocracoke Inlet** and killed in a desperate fight. Gov. Eden and other officials were thought to have been sharing in his profits from piracy.

Courtesy NCDA&H

July 25, 1729
The Lords Proprietors, except Earl Granville, sold their rights to the English Crown, and North Carolina became a **Royal Colony.** Granville retained property rights in much of the colony, marked off as the **Granville District,** until the American Revolution.

**The
Royal Colony**

**A Sea
of Troubles**

**The
Royal Colony**

**Elements
of Style**

January 15, 1730

January 31, 1734

September 1739

November 1746

August 26, 1747

October 1749

January 15, 1730
George Burrington, a prominent landowner, was commissioned as the first Royal Governor of North Carolina.

January 31, 1734
The first lots sold in **New Liverpool** (later Wilmington), located at the junction of the two branches of the Cape Fear River. Not a planned town, it drew a large number of people away from the Brunswick settlement.

September 1739
The first large group of **Highland Scots,** escaping from persecution by the British government, arrived and settled on the upper Cape Fear River, around the present-day **Fayette-ville** area.

November 1746
The Assembly, which met at Wilmington with no Albemarle delegates present (they had been detained by bad weather), chose New Bern as the colonial capital and voted to **equalize representa-tion** for all counties. The representation vote angered the powerful and heavily populated Albemarle counties, who boycotted the Assembly and refused to pay taxes for eight years. This created nearly a decade of almost complete lawlessness there, or as one North Carolinian put it, "fist law."

August 26, 1747
The Spanish briefly occupied Beaufort in the **War of Jenkins' Ear,** the British and Spanish Naval war fought on the high seas that began in 1737 over control of trade to the New World. Ocracoke, Core Sound and Brunswick also were attacked, but there were no casualties.

October 1749
Printer **James Davis** of New Bern published the first book printed in North Carolina, a journal of proceedings of the colony's legis-lature. Three years later, in 1751, he began publishing the first weekly newspaper printed in North Carolina, New Bern's *North Carolina Gazette.*

Courtesy NCDA&H

Courtesy NCDA&H

November 17, 1753

BETHABARA 1766

November 17, 1753
Moravians, an ancient Protestant Hussite denomination renewed in Germany in the 18th century, settled on a 100,000-acre tract in the northwestern piedmont area of North Carolina, naming it **Wachovia.** **Bethabara,** or Old Town, was their first planned town.

March 1754

March 1754
The English Grand Lodge licensed **St. John's of Wilmington** as North Carolina's first Masonic lodge. The Masons constituted the strongest fraternal organization in colonial North Carolina.

January 25, 1759

January 25, 1759
Illegal acts of Granville's land-agent, Francis Corbin, led to his kidnapping and caused the **Enfield Riot.** Corbin, who had over-charged taxes and pocketed the difference, was forced to reform and soon was dismissed from his post.

June 6, 1761

June 6, 1761
The French and Indian War, fought in North America between England and France over control of the Ohio Valley region, found its way to the western North Carolina frontier in a series of small battles, including a Cherokee Indian raid on **Ft. Dobbs** in Rowan County. A peace treaty was signed with the Cherokees on this date, and, once again, all was quiet on the western frontier.

January 1, 1764

January 1, 1764
New Bern Academy became the first chartered school in North Carolina.

November 16, 1765

January 1, 1766

February 19, 1766

1766

November 16, 1765
After citizens of New Hanover County had demonstrated against the **British Stamp Act** the previous month at Wilmington, they forced the resignation of the new stamp distributor for North Carolina, Dr. William Houston.

January 1, 1766
The Moravians founded **Salem** (now part of Winston-Salem), which became the major town in their progressive, self-contained community. This highly religious group promoted social discipline and harmony. Pictured at right is Salem's officially designated "First House," which has been reconstructed.

Courtesy Moravian Archives

April 1766
The British repealed the Stamp Act, and calm returned to North Carolina.

June 6, 1766
With western settlers seeking better regulation of eastern-controlled North Carolina government, Schoolmaster George Simms of Granville County issued the **"Nutbush Address."** He attacked local officials for collection of unfair fees and taxes and other illegal practices, and thus began the Regulator Movement.

February 19, 1766
The Wilmington protestors, now organized as the **Sons of Liberty,** marched to Brunswick and forced a British officer to release ships detained for lacking stamped papers. Although an armed protest, there was no violence as the protestors met with no resistance.

Courtesy NCDA&H

March 15, 1767　　November 1768　　September 24, 1770　　May 16, 1771　　September 25, 1773

November 1768
The town of **Charlotte,** named after the reigning Queen of England, was incorporated. It originally was a crossroads of two trails used heavily during westward settlement.

September 24, 1770
In the thinly settled areas of the western piedmont, **Regulators,** as the protestors came to be known, seized Hillsborough in a violent protest after the Assembly failed to pass laws to help the western settlers.

May 16, 1771
Fearing civil war between the eastern and western sections of North Carolina, **Gov. William Tryon,** who had been in office since 1765, deployed a well-trained military force of over 1,000 men to restore order in the west. The Regulators were soundly defeated, ending the **War of Regulation.**

Courtesy NCDA&H

March 15, 1767
Andrew Jackson, seventh President of the United States, was born in the Waxhaw region, near the North Carolina-South Carolina border.

Courtesy NCDA&H

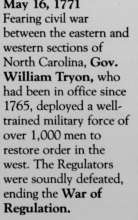

Courtesy NCDA&H

September 25, 1773
Frontiersman **Daniel Boone** left his Yadkin River home in Rowan County to begin exploration of Kentucky, blazing trails, including the Wilderness Road, for westward pioneers.

August 25, 1774
The first of five provincial congresses was established in North Carolina under the auspices of the **Continental Congress.** The purpose of this important colonywide assembly was to offer resistance to the British government by an organized group of popularly elected American colonists.

Courtesy NCDA&H

October 25, 1774
The Edenton Tea Party. In a public expression of protest of the British tax on East Indian Tea, 51 patriotic women from at least five North Carolina counties met at the home of Mrs. Elizabeth King in Edenton and signed a resolution vowing to drink no more of this popular drink.

April 8, 1775
Royal Gov. Josiah Martin dissolved the North Carolina legislature when, as another form of colonial protest, that body would not cooperate with him.

May 31, 1775
A committee of citizens from Mecklenburg County met at Charlotte Courthouse and adopted a set of 20 resolves, known as the **Mecklenburg Resolves,** protesting acts of the British government, voiding all British authority in the colony until abuses were corrected and calling for the election of military offices by the powers of the people. This was the strongest of early written protests leading up to the Revolutionary War.

February 27, 1776
In the **Battle of Moore's Creek Bridge,** Patriot militia, under the command of Col. James Moore and Col. Richard Caswell, overwhelmingly defeated Tory forces in the first important Revolutionary War battle in North Carolina and in the South. The Patriots' victory here upset the British plans to quickly overpower the Southern colonies, and it also forestalled any other invasion by the British forces for several years.

Courtesy NCDA&H

80

The War
for
Independence

April 12, 1776 | November 12, 1776 | December 24, 1776 | July 21, 1778 | September 19, 1778 | June 20, 1780

April 12, 1776
The fourth Provincial Congress met at Halifax and instructed North Carolina delegates to the **Continental Congress** to cast their vote for American independence from Britain.

November 12, 1776
The first state constitution for North Carolina was adopted by the Provincial Congress in Hillsborough.

Courtesy NCDA&H

December 24, 1776
Richard Caswell was elected the first governor of the state of North Carolina by the Provincial Congress. This later was ratified by the people.

July 21, 1778
John Penn, Cornelius Harnett and John Williams, North Carolina's delegates to the Continental Congress, signed the **Articles of Confederation** of the first national Constitution.

September 19, 1778
William Gaston, a Roman Catholic who became Chief Justice of the North Carolina Supreme Court, was born in New Bern. Gaston authored "The Old North State," which later was adopted as the official state song. Both Gaston County and the city of Gastonia were named for him.

June 20, 1780
Patriots under Col. Francis Locke and Maj. Joseph McDowell won the **Battle of Ramsour's Mill,** near Lincolnton, over Tories led by John Moore.

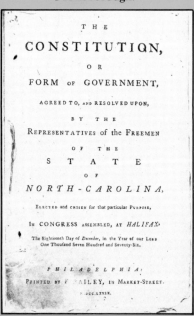

Courtesy North Carolina Collection

Courtesy NCDA&H

Courtesy NCDA&H

October 7, 1780
Cornwallis' Redcoats moving north from South Carolina were driven back by raw North Carolina militia at the **Battle of King's Mountain.** This Patriot victory delayed the planned British invasion of North Carolina.

January 28, 1781
British forces under Maj. James H. Craig occupied the **port of Wilmington,** which became an important supply base for the army of Cornwallis.

March 3, 1781
The Battle of Guilford Courthouse. Cornwallis won a victory here but paid a terrible price in dead and wounded. His army would never again be as powerful.

June 26, 1781
David Fanning, a daring Tory leader, seized Hillsborough and took prisoner **Gov. Thomas Burke** and members of his council. While Burke was a prisoner, North Carolina had no governing leader.

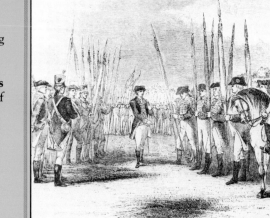

Courtesy NCDA&H

October 19, 1781
Cornwallis, hemmed into the Yorktown Peninsula by the French Navy and armies of **Washington** and **Lafayette,** surrendered.

Courtesy NCDA&H

The
Revolutionary
Epoch

North Carolina
and the
Nation

September 3, 1783   **August 23, 1784**   **July 21, 1788**   **November 21, 1789**   **December 11, 1789**   **February 25, 1790**

July 21, 1788
A state convention met
at Hillsborough to
consider the new
Federal Constitution
that had been adopted
in 1787 at the Consti-
tutional Convention
held in Philadelphia.
Alexander Martin
(depicted below), who
served two terms as
North Carolina's
governor, was a member
of that convention.
Fearing the **federal
government's power**
and because of the
absence of a **Bill of
Rights,** North Carolina
became one of only two
states, along with Rhode
Island, to reject the new
Constitution.

December 11, 1789
The North Carolina
General Assembly
chartered the
**University of North
Carolina,** which
opened at Chapel Hill
on January 15, 1795.

August 23, 1784
North Carolina counties
west of the Appalachians,
protesting neglect by the
state government,
formed a new state
called **Franklin.** The
idea collapsed when
backers could get
recognition from neither
North Carolina nor the
federal government.

February 25, 1790
North Carolina ceded to
the federal government
its territory between the
Appalachians and the
Mississippi, which
became the state of
Tennessee in 1794.
This constituted the last
major adjustment to
North Carolina's
borders.

September 3, 1783
The British agreed to a
peace treaty recog-
nizing **American
independence.**

Courtesy NCDA&H

November 21, 1789
Isolated from sister
states and promised that
a Bill of Rights would
be added to the
Constitution in due
course, a convention at
Cross Creek — later
renamed **Fayetteville**
after popular French
Gen. Marquis de
Lafayette — agreed to
accept it.

Courtesy NCDA&H

The Age
of the
Antifederalists

The
Jeffersonian
Years

March 30, 1792   **November 2, 1795**   **1799**   **August 15, 1800**   **August 1801**

November 2, 1795
James K. Polk, 11th
President of the United
States, was born in
Mecklenburg County.

1799
Conrad Reed made the
first authenticated
discovery of gold in the
nation, a 17-pound
nugget, in Cabarrus
County. This began
America's first "gold
rush," and North
Carolina became the
chief gold-mining state
for the next 50 years.

August 15, 1800
North Carolinians,
reacting to high-handed
acts of President **John
Adams'** Federalist
administration, voted
for **Thomas Jefferson's**
Antifederalist, or
Republican, platform.
Jefferson's presidency
began a 35-year period
of Republican control
of both the state and
national governments.

Courtesy NCDA&H

August 1801
The Great Revival,
spreading out from
Kentucky origins,
ignited in the Orange
County outdoor camp
meetings of the Rev.
William Paisley. It
quickly spread
throughout the state as
the greatest religious
movement in North
Carolina history.

Courtesy NCDA&H

March 30, 1792
Joel Lane, a prominent
farmer, sold his tract in
Wake County as the site
of North Carolina's
permanent capital,
Raleigh. Centrally
located, Wake County
was chosen as a
compromise between
new settlements in the
western part of the state
and the established ones
in the east. Pictured
above is the Joel Lane
house, which was
moved in 1927 to its
present location at 728
West Hargett Street in
Raleigh.

Courtesy NCDA&H

84

Courtesy NCDA&H

September 5, 1802
John Stanly of New Bern killed former **Gov. Richard Dobbs Spaight** (pictured above) in North Carolina's most celebrated duel. Efforts to outlaw the practice of dueling did not succeed.

November 18, 1805
North Carolina's Court of Conference was converted into the **North Carolina Supreme Court** by an act of the legislature.

March 12, 1808
The town of **Greensboro,** destined to become one of North Carolina's largest and most progressive cities, was founded.

December 29, 1808
Andrew Johnson, 17th President of the United States, was born in Raleigh.

Courtesy NCDA&H

June 2, 1802
A cryptic message found in a slave cabin in **Bertie County** about a planned uprising generated North Carolina's greatest conspiracy panic. Eleven slaves were executed in Bertie alone.

May 16, 1804
Salem Female Academy opened, launching higher education for women in North Carolina.

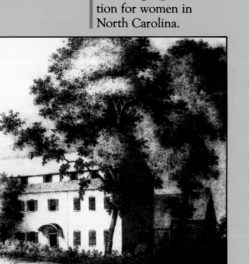

Courtesy NCDA&H

Courtesy NCDA&H

85

**The Age
of the
Antifederalists**

**The Rip Van
Winkle Years:
N.C. Asleep**

June 1814

September 12, 1818

1823

February 26, 1825

January 10, 1826

Courtesy NCDA&H

June 1814
During the War of
1812, **Johnston
Blakeley,** North
Carolina's most famous
Naval commander,
captained the **USS
Wasp,** shown below in
a sea battle with the
British ship, Reindeer.
Blakeley destroyed two
British ships in the
English channel before
his ship was lost at sea
on his attempt to return
home.

Courtesy Parramore Collection

**September 12, 1818
Richard J. Gatling,**
inventor of the first
successful machine gun
and numerous agricul-
tural implements, was
born in Hertford County
near Murfreesboro.

Courtesy NCDA&H

**1823
The Ocracoke Light-
house,** the oldest
continuously used
lighthouse in the state,
was built by the federal
government.

**February 26, 1825
General Lafayette,** on
tour of the Southern
states, spent the night at
the Indian Queen
Tavern in Murfreesboro,
his first overnight stop
in North Carolina. He
later visited such towns
as Halifax, Raleigh and
Fayetteville, his
namesake town.

January 10, 1826
Former **Gov. Benjamin
Smith** died at Smith-
ville (now Southport),
where he was in jail
for debt.

Courtesy NCDA&H

Courtesy NCDA&H

March 9, 1829	Summer 1829	March 26, 1830	June 21, 1831	July 1831	August 22, 1831

August 22, 1831
Nat Turner led the greatest slave insurrection in the history of the United States in Southampton County, Virginia, near the North Carolina line. Many North Carolina blacks were executed in the white panic that ensued. Turner and his cohorts were captured and executed, also.

Summer 1829
George Moses Horton published *The Hope of Liberty*, the first book of poetry by a North Carolinian. Horton was a Chatham County slave. Although efforts by interested people to buy Horton's freedom failed, he lived long enough to be freed as a result of the Civil War.

March 26, 1830
The state's Baptists had split into the Conservative and Progressive Wings, and the latter organized into the **Baptist State Convention** at Greenville. By this time, they were the largest denomination in North Carolina.

July 1831
Christopher and August Bechtler opened a private mint in the gold-mining region near Rutherfordton. They made the first gold dollar minted in the United States.

June 21, 1831
The State House in Raleigh with the famous **Canova** marble statue of Washington burned in a morning blaze.

March 9, 1829
John Branch of Halifax became the first North Carolinian to serve in a President's cabinet when Andrew Jackson appointed him Secretary of the Navy.

Courtesy NCDA&H

Courtesy Parramore Collection

January 1, 1833

January 1, 1833
The first railroad in the state opened. It was a temporary line that carried granite 1¼ miles from a quarry to the site of the new state Capitol in Raleigh. It carried passengers on outings as well on Sundays.

1833

1833
A North Carolina legislative committee reported that nine-tenths of the state's farmers would emigrate if they could, so backward was the state after years of penny-pinching, small government Democratic rule. Many already were moving west and south.

February 4, 1834

February 4, 1834
Wake Forest Institute (later Wake Forest University) was founded in Wake County by North Carolina Baptists. For men only, it was the state's first Baptist institution for higher learning.

Courtesy NCDA&H

June 4, 1835

June 4, 1835
At the Constitutional Convention in Raleigh, the **state constitution** was remade to balance western and eastern representation, since over half of the state's population of 738,000 now lived in the western part of the state. Because the State House had been burned in 1831, most of these sessions were held in Raleigh's First Presbyterian Church, pictured at left. The new state constitution also gave Roman Catholics equal rights as Protestants to hold office and lowered property qualifications for voting. Free blacks lost their right to vote, however, and non-Christians could not hold public office. Nevertheless, important advances in democracy and sectional fairness initiated a new era of progress in North Carolina.

December 31, 1835

Courtesy NCDA&H

December 31, 1835
Edward B. Dudley of New Hanover, the first Whig governor, took office. The new Whig party aimed at reform of certain political, economic and social conditions.

December 29, 1836

December 29, 1836
The Cherokee Indians, who had been driven into the southeast corner of the state, finally surrendered their last tribal lands to the federal government by the **Treaty of New Echota,** which nearly all Cherokees later renounced. Most of the tribe soon was forced to resettle on reservations in Oklahoma, although a number of Cherokees returned and hid out in their beloved mountains in western North Carolina.

Courtesy NCDA&H

March 1, 1837	August 6, 1837	December 1837	June 15, 1838	January 20, 1840	March 7, 1840

January 20, 1840
After the state legislature passed an act establishing common (free) schools in North Carolina, the first free school opened in **Rockingham County.** This act was one result of Whig control of the state government.

March 7, 1840
The Wilmington and Weldon Railroad, the longest in the world at 161½ miles, was completed. Because it ran north to south, it was a major link in connecting North Carolina with Northern states.

August 6, 1837
Quakers established the **New Garden Boarding School,** a coeducational institution, in Guilford County. Its name was changed in 1889 to **Guilford College.**

December 1837
The Charlotte Branch of the **United States Mint** opened. Prior to the Civil War, more than $5 million in gold from the North Carolina hills was minted here.

June 15, 1838
The Rev. John Chavis of Granville County, the brilliant black teacher and Presbyterian minister whose school in Raleigh had once served whites in the daytime and black scholars at night, died. Chavis was a veteran of Virginia forces in the Revolutionary War, and he had studied at Princeton College. At right is a copy of Chavis' August 25, 1808, advertisement in the *Raleigh Register* informing the public of his decision to segregate the students of his school by race.

March 1, 1837
Presbyterians founded **Davidson College** in Mecklenburg County. At first a manual labor school, it later was converted into a classical college.

Courtesy Chalmers G. Davidson, Davidson College

EDUCATION.

JOHN CHAVES takes this method of informing his Employers, and the Citizens of Raleigh in general, that the present Quarter of his School will end the 15th of September, and the next will commence on the 19th. He will, at the same time, open an EVENING SCHOOL for the purpose of instructing Children of Colour, as he intends, for the accommodation of some of his Employers, to exclude all Children of Colour from his Day School.

The Evening School will commence at an hour by Sun. When the white children leave the House, those of colour will take their places, and continue until ten o'clock

The terms of teaching the white children will be as usual, two and a half dollars per quarter; those of colour, one dollar and three quarters. In both cases, the whole of the money to be paid in advance to Mr. Benjamin S King. Those who produce Certificates from him of their having paid the money, will be admitted.

Those who think proper to put their Children under his care, may rely upon the strictest attention being paid not only to their Education but to their Morals which he deems an *important* part of Education. Aug 23, 1808.

He hopes to have a better School House by the commencement of the next quarter

Courtesy NCDA&H

| March 5, 1841 | February 2, 1847 | January 29, 1849 | July 9, 1850 | April 18, 1853 | October 18, 1853 |

Courtesy NCDA&H

July 9, 1850
William A. Graham
of Lincoln County was
appointed Secretary of
the Navy in Zachary
Taylor's cabinet.

Courtesy NCDA&H

March 5, 1841
George E. Badger of
New Bern, a founding
leader of the Whig party
in North Carolina, was
appointed Secretary of
the Navy in President
John Tyler's cabinet.

February 2, 1847
A regiment of the
**North Carolina
Volunteers** left for war
in Mexico. Because the
national Whig party
failed to give full
support to this war and
the acquisition of
Mexican land, it began
to lose its influence.

January 29, 1849
Construction of the
**State Hospital of the
Insane,** the first
hospital of its kind in
the state, was begun in
Raleigh. Dorothea Dix
of Massachusetts had
lobbied successfully for
it with the state
legislature. It opened
in 1856.

April 18, 1853
Former Vice President
William Rufus King
of Sampson County
died. He had been in
office under President
James Monroe.

October 18, 1853
The first annual **State
Fair** opened at Raleigh.
It soon became a
popular event for
exhibiting prize
agricultural and
industrial products of
Tar Heels. Pictured
below is the sterling
silver medal awarded for
"Best in Show."

Courtesy NCDA&H

Courtesy NCDA&H

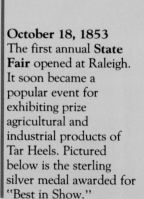

Courtesy NCDA&H

| April 17, 1854 | January 1, 1856 | January 23, 1857 | May 20, 1861 | June 10, 1861 | August 29, 1861 |

January 1, 1856
The state owned and
financed **North Caro-
lina Railroad** was
completed between
Charlotte and
Goldsboro. This became
the single most
important economic
step in the history of the
state to date as its route
spanned what came to
be known as the
Piedmont Crescent of
major population
centers.

April 17, 1854
The world's longest
plank road, over 100
miles from Fayetteville
to Salem, North
Carolina, was com-
pleted. Although
considered a major step
toward all-weather roads
at the time, plank roads
later were abandoned as
too expensive to
maintain. Pictured is a
plank road passenger
toll ticket.

January 23, 1857
Northampton County
native **Miles Darden,**
the "World's Largest
Man" at 7 feet 6 inches
and over 1,000 pounds,
died in Tennessee.

May 20, 1861
Six weeks after the Civil
War began, the Seces-
sion Convention at
Raleigh passed the
**Ordinance of
Secession.** By this act,
North Carolina became
the last state to join the
Confederacy.

Courtesy NCDA&H

June 10, 1861
Henry L. Wyatt of
Edgecomb County was
killed at the Battle of Big
Bethel, Virginia. He was
the first Confederate
soldier killed in action.
Although little major
fighting was done on
North Carolina soil
during the Civil War,
North Carolina had
more troops in this war
and lost more men than
any other state.

August 29, 1861
Easily overcoming state
troops, Union troops
captured **Forts Hatteras
and Clark** on the
Outer Banks.

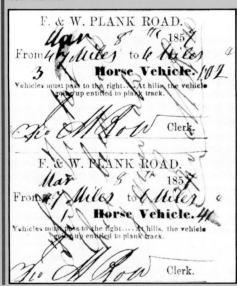

Courtesy NCDA&H

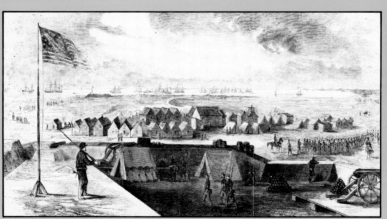

Courtesy North Carolina Collection

February 20, 1862
Union forces burned
Winton in revenge for
a Confederate ambush
there the day before.
Winton was the first
town burned in the
Civil War.

Courtesy North Carolina Collection

March 14, 1862
Union forces occupied
New Bern in the first
Union conquest on
North Carolina's
mainland.

September 8, 1862
At the age of 32, **Col.
Zebulon B. Vance,**
destined to become the
most popular political
leader in the state's
history, was elected
governor while
commanding troops.
Although a strong
Unionist, Vance served
as a Confederate Army
officer because, "If war
should come, I prefer
to be with my own
people." Below, Vance
is portrayed at right in
this painting of the
26th North Carolina
Regiment colonels,
along with Col. H. K.
Burgwin (center) and
Col. J. R. Lane (left).

Courtesy NCDA&H

September 11, 1862
**William Sidney
Porter,** the celebrated
American writer of
short stories under the
pseudonym **O. Henry,**
was born in Guilford
County.

February 8, 1862
The Burnside Expedition destroyed North
Carolina Naval forces
and captured Roanoke
Island, the key to the
eastern river system. It
was becoming more and
more difficult for
Confederates to use
North Carolina's ports.

Courtesy North Carolina Collection

Courtesy NCDA&H

92

December 30, 1862

Courtesy NCDA&H

**December 30, 1862
The USS Monitor,** the Union ironclad, sank in a gale off Cape Hatteras while being towed to South Carolina. Earlier, it had engaged the Confederate ship, Virginia, to a draw in the first battle in history between ironclad ships. Over 100 years later, the USS Monitor became the first marine sanctuary in the state.

1863

January 1, 1863
Abraham Lincoln's **Emancipation Proclamation** took effect, freeing slaves in seceded states. It was a "paper" emancipation for most slaves, however, who had to wait for the Confederacy to be defeated to receive their freedom.

**July 3, 1863
Gen. J. J. Pettigrew's** North Carolina troops went "farthest" up Cemetery Ridge of any Confederate troops at the **Battle of Gettysburg.** The Confederate failure in this battle was a major turning point in the Civil War. Pictured is the North Carolina Monument at Gettysburg National Military Park, Gettysburg, Pennsylvania.

Jerry Cotten Photo

April 24, 1864

April 24, 1864
In one of the few Confederate victories in North Carolina, Plymouth was recaptured from the Union by **Gen. Robert F. Hoke** with the assistance of a new ram, the Albemarle.

October 27, 1864

October 27, 1864
A Union Naval force under Lt. William Cushing sank **the ram Albemarle** at Plymouth wharf in a night raid. This powerful ram had been counted on to relieve the pressure of the Union blockade of the North Carolina coast.

Courtesy NCDA&H

March 4, 1865
Gen. William T. Sherman's army entered North Carolina after devastating Georgia and South Carolina. The easy victories of this great Union force at Fayetteville (pictured), Kinston and Averasboro were sure signs that the Confederacy was collapsing.

Courtesy North Carolina Collection

January 15, 1865
Fort Fisher, the largest earthwork fort in the world and key to Cape Fear River defense, fell to Union forces opening the way to Union occupation of Wilmington, the Confederacy's last major port.

Courtesy NCDA&H

March 19-21, 1865
Sherman defeated Gen. Joseph E. Johnston's army at the **Battle of Bentonville,** the bloodiest battle ever fought on North Carolina soil. A total of 4,000 men from both sides died in the action.

Courtesy NCDA&H

April 13, 1865
Sherman's army occupied Raleigh.

April 14, 1865
Vice President Andrew Johnson, a native of Raleigh who had risen to political prominence in Tennessee before the war, became President of the United States at the death of Abraham Lincoln.

**The Death
and Revival of
Conservative Rule**

April 26, 1865	December 1, 1865	March 1866	March 2, 1867	January 14, 1868

January 14, 1868
A Republican-dominated state convention adopted a new state constitution that abolished slavery, ended the last religious and property qualifications for office and voting, and extended the governor's term from two to four years, among other changes. With this new constitution, **North Carolina returned to the Union** after seven years of secession.

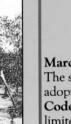

Courtesy NCDA&H

March 1866
The state legislature adopted the **Black Code,** which gave limited rights of citizenship to Negroes. Blacks were not allowed to vote, however, nor could they testify in court against whites or enjoy certain other rights of white citizens.

March, 2, 1867
Radicals in power in Congress placed North Carolina and other former Confederate states under martial law and began to institute a more radical phase of **Reconstruction.** Because President Johnson sought mild treatment of Southern whites, many Northerners felt he was throwing away the chance to make major reforms in the South.

April 26, 1865
Gen. Johnston surrendered his army — the last major Confederate force still in the field — at **Bennett Place in Durham.** Gen. Robert E. Lee's Northern Virginia army previously had surrendered at Appomattox Courthouse, Virginia, on April 9th.

**December 1, 1865
Shaw University** opened in Raleigh for the education of Freedmen, as former slaves were known.

Courtesy NCDA&H

Courtesy NCDA&H

| July 20, 1868 | March 7, 1870 | December 14, 1870 | February 17, 1872 | January 16, 1874 | October 19, 1874 |

July 20, 1868
The North Carolina delegation was admitted to the **U.S. Congress.**

Courtesy NCDA&H

March 7, 1870
Ku Klux Klan activity caused Gov. W. W. Holden to place several counties under martial law. The KKK sought to intimidate blacks to keep them from voting and other activities.

December 14, 1870
Gov. William W. Holden (pictured below) was impeached by conservatives in the state legislature. He was convicted of "crimes and misdemeanors" and was replaced as governor on March 22, 1871, by Tod R. Caldwell. Gradually, the old white power structure of the prewar years was regaining its influence.

Courtesy NCDA&H

February 17, 1872
The Board of Trustees of the University of North Carolina voted to admit white women. This was a major gain for women, who previously had been denied equal educational opportunities with men.

January 16, 1874
Chang and Eng Bunker, Siamese twins joined at the chest, died in Wilkes County, where they had built a home and married sisters. They were more widely known than **Millie-Christine,** Negro Siamese twins joined at the hip, who lived in what is now Columbus County.

October 19, 1874
Richard J. Reynolds bought property in Winston on which he built a plant for the manufacture of chewing tobacco. Today, R. J. Reynolds Industries is North Carolina's largest corporation.

Courtesy NCDA&H

Industrial
and Economic
Progress

October 3, 1879   April 30, 1884   January 1887   April 20, 1887   October 3, 1889

January 1887
The State Department of Labor was established, an important gain for North Carolina's industrial workers.

April 20, 1887
The first chapter of the **Farmer's Alliance** in the state was formed in Robeson County. By organizing, American farmers in revolt against business-oriented government, railroad monopolies and other problems hoped to find solutions.

October 3, 1879
The **first telephone exchange** in the state was opened at Raleigh. Other cities quickly followed, including the telephone exchange office pictured here in Wilson.

Courtesy NCDA&H

October 3, 1889
The North Carolina College of Agriculture and Mechanics (now N.C. State University) opened as a land grant college at Raleigh with 72 students. Pictured is Holladay Hall, the first building erected on the campus.

Courtesy North Carolina Collection

April 30, 1884
Bonsack cigarette-making machines were installed at Duke and Bull Durham factories in Durham. Replacing hand-rolled cigarettes, these machines manufactured 1,000 cigarettes a day. By this time, tobacco, textiles and furniture-making dominated the state's industry.

Courtesy NCDA&H

| January 31, 1890 | September 2, 1892 | October 5, 1892 | November 1892 | November 6, 1894 | November 3, 1896 |

**October 5, 1892
Normal and Industrial School** opened at Greensboro after a campaign by the Farmer's Alliance. At first a teachers college for women, it later became the coeducational University of North Carolina at Greensboro.

**September 2, 1892
Trinity College** moved from Randolph County to Durham after big gifts from industrialists Washington Duke and Julian S. Carr. Trinity College later became Duke University.

November 6, 1894
Republicans joined forces with the new People's party to defeat the Democrats. Called **Fusionists,** this new alliance represented the farmer-worker protest against years of white conservative domination.

Courtesy NCDA&H

November 3, 1896
With the reform movement still powerful, Fusionists again defeated the Democrats. Republican **Daniel Russell** won the governor's race, with strong backing from the state's black voters.

**January 31, 1890
James B. Duke** of Durham organized the **American Tobacco Company** and created a virtual monopoly over the tobacco industry. Duke, photographed here as a young man, was the son of Washington Duke, a tobacco farmer who revolutionized the industry when he turned his harvests into smoking tobacco and began selling it from a wagon. Prior to its breakup in 1911, the American Tobacco Company would become the world's largest tobacco producer.

Courtesy NCDA&H

November 1892
Protesting farmers, after organizing themselves into a union, joined the new **People's** (Populist) party and elected several members to the state legislature. The **Farmer's Revolt** was in high gear in both the state and the nation.

Courtesy North Carolina Collection

| April 27, 1898 | May 11, 1898 | September 1, 1898 | November 2, 1898 | November 10, 1898 |

September 1, 1898
The first forestry school in the United States was opened by **Dr. Carl Schenck** in Biltmore Forest near Asheville. **George W. Vanderbilt,** Schenck's sponsor, owned the Biltmore Forest and the enormous mansion of the same name nearby.

Courtesy NCDA&H

April 27, 1898
Gov. Russell authorized the creation of a black battalion under **Maj. James Young,** a black Wake County legislator who edited the *Raleigh Gazette* from 1893 to 1898. Later promoted to colonel, Young organized the **Third North Carolina Regiment** (pictured below).

May 11, 1898
Ensign Worth Bagley of Raleigh was the first Naval officer killed in the Spanish-American War. This war resulted in the United States acquiring much of Spain's former colonial empire.

Courtesy NCDA&H

November 10, 1898
Red Shirts were involved in the **Wilmington Race Riots,** in which 10 blacks were killed and black and other Republican officials were forcibly removed from local offices.

November 2, 1898
Democrats, campaigning mainly on the race issue, beat the Fusionists and returned to political control of the state. The agrarian protest movement by this time was in decline, and mounted vigilantes, known as **Red Shirts,** prevented blacks from voting in some areas.

Courtesy NCDA&H

99

March 4, 1899

April 1, 1899

August 2, 1900

January 15, 1901

August 1, 1901

March 4, 1899
State law required
railroad and steamship
lines to provide separate
accommodations for
blacks and whites. **"Jim
Crow" legislation**
segregated races in most
public facilities by this
time.

**April 1, 1899
The North Carolina
Mutual Life
Insurance Company,**
destined to become one
of the nation's largest
black-owned businesses,
was formed in Durham.
Pictured below along
with a group of
prominent black
businessmen are C.C.
Spaulding (fourth from
left, front row) and
John Merrick (fifth
from right, middle
row), two of the
organizers of the
company. Booker T.
Washington sits in the
center, middle row.

August 2, 1900
North Carolina voters
adopted the **"Grand-
father Clause"** as an
amendment to the state
constitution. Its effect
was to deny most black
citizens the right to vote
or hold office.

Courtesy NCDA&H

**January 15, 1901
Charles B. Aycock** was
inaugurated as governor.
Aycock's emphasis on
improving North
Carolina's backward
school system gave him
the reputation of the
state's "Education
Governor." His efforts
were part of a national
reform called the
Progressive Movement.

August 1, 1901
New Bern drugstore
owner **Caleb D.
Bradham** began using
the **Pepsi-Cola**
trademark for the
beverage he concocted
at New Bern in the
1890s. Bradham went
bankrupt, but his drink
became a national
favorite. Pictured below
is the trademark that
Bradham filed with the
Secretary of State, State
of North Carolina, on
June 23, 1896, for his
beverage.

Courtesy North Carolina Collection

Pep-Kola

Courtesy NCDA&H

November 1902
Walter Clark was elected Chief Justice of the North Carolina Supreme Court. A leading progressive, Clark helped modernize the Court and fought for women's rights, labor's right to organize, workmen's compensation, an end to lynchings and other progressive goals. He died in 1924.

December 17, 1903
Wilbur and Orville Wright, bicycle mechanics from Ohio, made the first successful power-driven airplane flight from Kill Devil Hill at Kitty Hawk on the North Carolina coast.

January 1, 1909
Statewide **Prohibition** took effect under the **Turlington Act.** North Carolina was one of several states to enact Prohibition before it became national in 1920.

1909
The **4-H Club** was founded in Hertford County. Originally called the Corn Club because its members were boys trying to produce better corn, the 4-H Club became important in spreading information about better farming and homemaking. The 4 H's stand for head, hands, heart and health.

August 11, 1909
The **first SOS message** was sent by the liner, **Arapahoe,** sinking off Cape Hatteras. Stations like the **Weather Bureau at Cape Hatteras** (below) received such distress signals. Other duties of the Weather Bureau included weather observation, recording of climatological data and display of storm warnings.

February 23, 1911
The General Assembly established **Avery County.** It was the last county formed, making 100 in all.

Courtesy NCDA&H

Courtesy North Carolina Collection

May 29, 1911

March 5, 1913

March 1914

March 9, 1915

September 23, 1916

May 29, 1911
The U.S. Supreme Court declared the American Tobacco Company a monopoly in the restraint of trade and forced it to break up into five companies. Anti-monopoly efforts were a key aim of the **Progressive Movement.**

March 5, 1913
Josephus Daniels, editor of the Raleigh *News & Observer,* was named as Woodrow Wilson's Secretary of the Navy. President Wilson's administration was the first since the Civil War to include many Southerners in high office. Daniels later was Ambassador to Mexico.

Courtesy NCDA&H

RUTH IN FAYETTEVILLE—Here is the first picture ever made of Babe Ruth as a professional ballplayer. It was taken in Fayetteville, the day the great "Bambino" launched his career as a member of the Baltimore Orioles, by hitting a home run.

Courtesy NCDA&H

March 1914
George Herman Ruth hit his first professional home run in Fayetteville, the same city in which he acquired his nickname — Babe.

March 9, 1915
Election by **Australian (secret) ballot** was adopted by an act of the state Assembly. Balloting formerly had been done by show of hand or other public indication of choice.

Courtesy NCDA&H

September 23, 1916
Kiffen Rockwell of Asheville was killed in action in Europe. A member of the Lafayette Escadrille, Rockwell was the first American pilot to shoot down an enemy plane in World War I. Although the United States was not yet in the war, some Americans already had volunteered to fight on the side of Great Britain and France.

102

| April 6, 1917 | August 6, 1918 | August 16, 1918 | September 29, 1918 | October 1918 |

August 16, 1918
The Mirlo, a British tanker, was sunk off Rodanthe by a German submarine. The crew was rescued by **Chicamacomico Coast Guardsmen.**

Courtesy NCDA&H

April 6, 1917
Congress declared war on Germany. By midsummer, Camp Green, a military training base in Charlotte, was under construction. The first of three such camps built in the state during the war, Camp Green contained 2,000 buildings which provided for 50,000 troops. A total of 100,000 North Carolinians enlisted during World War I.

August 6, 1918
A German submarine sank the **Diamond Shoals Lightship** off the North Carolina coast.

September 29, 1918
North Carolina units of the **30th or Old Hickory Division** were involved in the attack against Germany's Hindenburg Line. The German defenses were beginning to crumble.

October 1918
An **influenza epidemic** swept the state, killing hundreds and closing public places in many cities.

October 30, 1919
The American Legion, an organization of veterans of American military forces, held its first convention in the state at Raleigh.

Courtesy NCDA&H

| August 1920 | November 2, 1920 | November 8, 1921 | December 8, 1924 | February 19, 1925 |

Courtesy NCDA&H

December 8, 1924
The James B. Duke
Endowment of $40
million was announced
for **Trinity College** —
whose name was
changed to Duke
University — and other
purposes. It was the
largest endowment
made anywhere up to
that time for educational
purposes. Pictured are
the members of the
board of trustees of
Trinity College.

August 1920
North Carolina rejected
the **19th amendment,**
which extended equal
voting rights to women.
The following day,
Tennessee passed the
amendment, giving it
the necessary two-thirds
majority of states.

November 8, 1921
Miss Exum Clement
of Asheville became the
first woman elected to
the General Assembly.

February 19, 1925
The House of Represent-
atives rejected a bill to
forbid teaching
evolution in the state's
public schools. Many
North Carolinians feared
that belief in evolution
might undermine faith
in God and the Bible.

November 2, 1920
Women voted for the
first time in North
Carolina's history.

Courtesy NCDA&H

Courtesy NCDA&H

104

May 22, 1926 | March 8, 1927 | January 1929 | June 1929 | October 29, 1929 | March 26, 1931

June 1929
A number of bitter, violent **strikes by North Carolina's textile workers** were felt throughout the state. These strikes failed, and, consequently, organized labor made very little progress during the months leading up to the Depression.

January 1929
The unusually strong and competent leadership of **Gov. O. Max Gardner** (1929-1933), pictured below at right with former Gov. Cameron Morrison (1921-1925), enabled North Carolinians to ease through the first years of the Depression without widespread panic.

March 8, 1927
Children under 16 years of age were forbidden by state law to work more than eight hours a day in factories.

Courtesy North Carolina Collection

March 26, 1931
In an economy move caused by the effects of the Great Depression, the University of North Carolina, N.C. State College and N.C. College for Women merged into the **Greater University of North Carolina.**

**October 29, 1929
The stock market crashed,** and the effects were devastating to the economy of the state. From January 1930 to January 1932, 131 state banks failed in North Carolina alone. In 1930, 70,000 North Carolinians were unemployed, and by the end of that year, it was apparent that the Great Depression was in high gear.

May 22, 1926
Congress established the **Great Smoky Mountains National Park,** thereby preserving millions of acres in the North Carolina mountains from commercial development.

Courtesy NCDA&H

105

| March 1932 | September 3, 1934 | November 12, 1934 | May 11, 1935 | July 1, 1937 | July 4, 1937 |

May 11, 1935
Although the **18th Amendment** had been revoked in 1933 as largely unenforceable, it was not until this date that the North Carolina General Assembly passed the local-option liquor sales act to end a quarter of a century of Prohibition in the state. The act was ratified the following February.

November 12, 1934
Congress authorized construction of the **Blue Ridge Parkway** to connect the Shenandoah Park in Virginia with the Great Smoky Mountains National Park. This highway became a boon to towns throughout North Carolina. Pictured is a viaduct, a long bridge over a gorge or valley, under construction along the parkway.

March 1932
The North Carolina Symphony Society was inaugurated at Chapel Hill. In 1943, the state appropriated money for the Symphony.

September 3, 1934
Scores of **textile mills closed** as Tar Heel workers joined the national walkout. Hard hit by the Depression, workers were seeking better wages and improvements in their working conditions.

July 1, 1937
The new state labor law took effect, fixing maximums of 10-hour work days and 55-hour work weeks for men (nine and 48 for women). It affected about 200,000 workers, after exceptions. The new child labor law also was in effect.

Courtesy NCDA&H

July 4, 1937
"Lost Colony," by Bladen County native **Paul Green,** was performed at Fort Raleigh for the first time. It tells the story of Sir Walter Raleigh's second Roanoke Island colony, which disappeared in 1587.

Courtesy NCDA&H

Courtesy NCDA&H

August 17, 1937 **September 15, 1938** **October 17, 1940** **April 5, 1941** **December 6, 1941**

October 17, 1940
With war raging in
Europe, the United
States established a
**Coast Guard air base
at Elizabeth City** to
guard against Nazi
submarines and other
enemy activities off the
North Carolina coast.
The state's selective
service draft quota was
set at 15,613 by
June 15, 1941.

April 5, 1941
Fort Raleigh on
Roanoke Island was
designated as **Fort
Raleigh National
Historic Site,** which
helped make the area an
important tourist
attraction.

Courtesy NCDA&H

August 17, 1937
**Cape Hatteras
National Seashore** was
established, a step
toward preserving parts
of North Carolina's
coastline from
commercial exploitation.

December 6, 1941
The Liberty Ship,
Zebulon B. Vance,
was launched at
Wilmington. It was the
first of 250 ships built
there during World
War II.

September 15, 1938
Asheville native and
UNC graduate **Thomas
Wolfe,** author of *Look
Homeward, Angel* and
other widely celebrated
novels, died in
Baltimore. He is
pictured above with his
mother at the family
home in Asheville.

Courtesy NCDA&H

Courtesy NCDA&H

107

April 1942
The British ship, San Delfino, was sunk by a German submarine north of Diamond Lightship Station Buoy. Bodies from this and other British ships sunk about the same time were interred at **The British Cemetery at Cape Hatteras.** By this time, a great many Tar Heels had served in the European and Pacific war zones. In August 1976, the cemetery was leased officially in perpetuity to the British government for the sum of one dollar.

March 4, 1943
The General Assembly adopted the **cardinal** as the state bird.

Courtesy NCDA&H

April 3, 1946
Thomas Dixon, lawyer, outdoorsman and author of *The Clansman*, the 1905 novel on which the full-length feature film, "The Birth of a Nation," was based, died at Raleigh. Both the book and the movie documented the KKK racist activities in the years following the Civil War.

January 1, 1942
In the **Rose Bowl** held at Durham because of war threats on the West Coast, Oregon State defeated Duke, 20-16. Duke's football team had gone undefeated during the regular season.

June 1, 1945
The total number of North Carolinians registered by local draft boards reached 1,137,276. Pictured above are the men of the **Thirtieth Infantry Division**, to which a large number of North Carolinians were assigned. This division fought in Europe, Asia, Africa and the Pacific islands.

Courtesy Duke University Archives

Halstead Collection

**Gains
and Losses**

**Civil Rights
and Wrongs**

October 19, 1948	June 27, 1952	August 1954	October 15, 1954	April 1956	January 18, 1958

**April 1956
The North Carolina
Museum of Art,** with
a state appropriation of
$1 million and the Kress
Foundation of New
York's art gift of
matching value, opened
in the old Highway
Building in Raleigh.

**January 18, 1958
Lumbee Indians**
invaded a Ku Klux Klan
rally, staged near
Maxton to intimidate
Robeson County
Indians, and chased off
hooded Klansmen.

October 19, 1948
President Harry S.
Truman spoke at the
unveiling of the **Three-
Presidents Statue**
(Jackson, Polk, A.
Johnson) on the Capitol
grounds in Raleigh.
Many North
Carolinians served in
high positions in
Truman's adminis-
tration. Pictured below
at the unveiling
ceremonies are (left to
right): Capus Waynick,
Willis Smith, President
Truman, Gov. R. Gregg
Cherry, Kenneth C.
Royall, Sen. Clyde R.
Hoey and Sen. William
B. Umstead.

**June 27, 1952
Kermit Hunter's**
drama, "Horn in the
West," premiered at
Boone.

August 1954
In light of the U.S.
Supreme Court's ruling
against segregated public
schools, Gov. Umstead
created the Advisory
Board to make
recommendations. The
resulting **Pearsall Plan**
established token
integration as North
Carolina's response.

**October 15, 1954
Hurricane Hazel**
smashed the North
Carolina coast with 150-
mile winds and 18-foot
tides, killing at least 19
and causing damages of
over $60 million. It
killed some 600 more as
it coursed northward
along the Atlantic
seaboard as far as
Labrador.

Courtesy NCDA&H

Courtesy NCDA&H

Courtesy NCDA&H

109

May 1958
Gov. Luther Hodges announced that Astra, Inc., a consulting and physics organization, would become the first tenant of the new **Research Triangle** in Wake, Orange and Durham counties. The Triangle rapidly developed into one of the nation's major research centers.

February 1, 1960
Four students from Greensboro's black Agricultural and Technical College staged a **sit-in at a Woolworth's** white-only lunch counter. This demonstration touched off a wave of similar ones throughout the South, resulting in the destruction of many racial barriers.

October 1960
The USS North Carolina, the 35,000-ton veteran battleship of every major Pacific engagement of World War II, was brought to Wilmington and converted to a tourist attraction — the USS North Carolina Battleship Memorial.

January 5, 1961
Terry Sanford was inaugurated as North Carolina's 31st governor. He had been warned by his advisors that his chances of being elected governor were in jeopardy because of his support of John F. Kennedy as the Democratic Presidential nominee when the majority of the southern delegates supported Lyndon Baines Johnson. Undaunted, Sanford continued to campaign for Kennedy, delivering a seconding address at Kennedy's nomination for the presidency in July 1960 at the Democratic National Convention in Los Angeles.

Courtesy Parramore Collection

March 1962
Judge Susie M. Sharp of Reidsville became the first female to be appointed an Associate Justice of the North Carolina Supreme Court. In 1974, she became the nation's first popularly elected female Chief Justice.

Courtesy Greensboro News & Record

Hugh Morton Photo

110

September 10, 1961	June 1963	January 8, 1965	November 5, 1968	January 3, 1969

June 1963
North Carolina's General Assembly enacted the notorious **Speaker Ban Law,** which banned radical speakers from state university campuses and other public property. The uproar that followed led to the act being found unconstitutional by a federal court in 1968.

January 8, 1965
Daniel K. Moore was sworn in as governor. Under his administration, North Carolina adopted the highly publicized **"brown bagging"** law that allowed patrons to bring their own alcohol into designated locations.

Courtesy Tant Studio

September 10, 1961
Ninteen-year-old Asheville native **Maria Beale Fletcher** became the first Miss North Carolina to be crowned Miss America.

November 5, 1968
Henry E. Frye of Guilford County became the first black in the North Carolina General Assembly in the 20th century. He became an Associate Justice of the State Supreme Court in 1983.

January 3, 1969
Gov. **Robert Scott** was inaugurated. During his term of office, North Carolinian's saw the first tax ever on tobacco, the first appropriation for the state zoo and reorganization of the state government administration and university system.

Fletcher Collection

Courtesy NCDA&H

111

May 6, 1969

February 6, 1971

November 7, 1972

November 8, 1977

January 10, 1981

May 6, 1969
Howard N. Lee was elected mayor of Chapel Hill and became the first black elected mayor of a predominantly white Southern town. In 1977, Lee was appointed State Secretary of Natural Resources and Community Development.

Courtesy Wilmington Journal

February 6, 1971
Despite recanting witnesses, nine blacks and one white were convicted of fire-bombing a grocery during racial violence at Wilmington. Gov. Hunt subsequently reduced the 282 years of imprisonment given to the "**Wilmington 10.**" The case gave the North Carolina court system widespread adverse publicity.

November 2, 1972
James E. Holshouser, Jr. (right, with former Gov. Robert Scott) became the first Republican to be elected governor of North Carolina in the 20th century. After generations of solid support for the Democrats, the South appeared to be on its way to becoming a two-party region.

November 8, 1977
North Carolinians adopted a constitutional amendment allowing the governor and lieutenant governor to serve two terms in office.

January 10, 1981
Gov. **James B. Hunt, Jr.**, was sworn in by North Carolina Supreme Court Chief Justice Joseph Branch. Hunt became the first governor since 1866 to be elected to two consecutive terms in office. **James C. Green** was sworn in as lieutenant governor, and he became the first to hold that office for two terms since it was created in 1868.

Courtesy Governors Office

Courtesy NCDA&H

112

March 29, 1982	April 4, 1983	August 30, 1983	November 22, 1983	July 13, 1984

August 30, 1983
William E. Thornton
of Faison became the
first Tar Heel astronaut
in space aboard the
week-long Challenger
space-shuttle mission.

November 22, 1983
Elizabeth II, a
reproduction of the
16th century sailing
vessel, was launched at
Manteo as part of North
Carolina's celebration of
the 400th anniversary of
the beginnings of
English America at
Roanoke Island.

July 13, 1984
On the **400th anniver-
sary** of the landing of
Sir Walter Raleigh's first
expedition on Roanoke
Island, the three-year
celebration of America's
400th anniversary
officially began. As the
first major commemor-
ative event of this
celebration, the
Elizabeth II was
commissioned and
opened for tours in
Manteo on Roanoke
Island. The nearby
Visitor Center for the
purpose of inter-
pretation of the ship
was also opened to the
public on this date.

Hugh Morton Photo

March 29, 1982
**The University of
North Carolina**
basketball team, behind
the heroics of Michael
Jordan, won the
national title, beating
Georgetown University
in the NCAA finals.
UNC previously had
won this title, in their
unbeaten year of 1957.

April 4, 1983
**North Carolina State
University** succeeded
UNC as the national
basketball champions,
defeating the University
of Houston. Successful
college teams have
turned North
Carolinians into avid
basketball and football
fans.

Courtesy N.C. Travel & Tourism

Courtesy Chip Henderson Photography

113

State of the State

CHAPTER 4

The Soul of a People

BY JOHN EHLE

Many people in North Carolina used to claim playing the fiddle was of the devil. Of course, it doubtless very often was. Regardless, music was socially the most acceptable of the performing arts; it was even used in churches. Drama was only sometimes acceptable; it helped if the plays were performed out of doors. Dance was not acceptable, indoors or out.

Over the years, these attitudes have changed, and we have come to view artists, painters, sculptors, singers and actors as human beings engaged in useful work. When I grew up in Asheville, there was only one resident who had performed professionally, a singer, and she was catered to wherever she went and was called "Madam." Today, artists multiply and even threaten to overtake other professions, except those of the lawyer and the highway patrolman.

The most complex of the state's arts communities is at Winston-Salem, where fifty organizations are part of the Arts Council. Located there, also is the N.C. School of the Arts, with students from all over the country admitted by competitive audition and instructed by professional performing artists. The performing arts are the most challenging of the arts to try to manipulate or manage since they require many people and many specialities, often even a combination of arts. The first act of the school was to cast about all over the country for the best performing artists in music, voice, dance and acting—and to make them the faculty. Of course, this is the best European method, the conservatory method; nothing new, but to us it was a revolution.

Since then, this faculty has taught hundreds of artists, and some members and graduates have started independent companies in music, dance and drama in North Carolina and other places and many in Winston-Salem itself, near the mother school.

We have rural arts communities, too, largely in the crafts. One built over the years is situated on a mountain ridge at Penland, near Burnsville. Penland School of Crafts offers classes to adults who want to work with wood, clay, metal, yarn, precious stones, glass and photography. The studios are open day and night, and instructors are professional craftspeople who come from all over the country to teach there. A number of other craftspeople have settled nearby; perhaps twenty studios are found along rural roads, set back in coves and at high places along the river.

A musician or actor needs others of his kind to play with him, and applaud, but a painter or craftsman—or a writer, for that matter—can be part of a community or be free of one or move from one to another. In

One of the three founders of the North Carolina School of the Arts, Ehle has been involved in many of the state's arts programs. A novelist, his recent book, *The Winter People,* received the Lillian Smith Award as best novel by a Southerner in 1982. Four of his novels have won the North Carolina prize for fiction. Ehle's latest novel, *Last One Home,* will be published by Harper and Row in the fall of 1984.

a real sense, there is no North Carolina or Kentucky or Pennsylvania artist. I have visited North Carolina-born writers Leon Rooke, at home in Victoria, British Columbia, Jonathan Williams in Yorkshire, England, Laurence Ferlinghetti in California. I have visited the late Harry Golden of New York in his home in Charlotte, the late Carl Sandburg of Chicago at his farm in Flat Rock, Maya Angelou of New York at her home just down the road. We export artists, import them. They move about. And we grow our own. A neighbor came by this morning to introduce his family's problem: His three children have turned out to be an

actress, a painter and a medical doctor who intends to practice medicine in order to write novels.

Among our arts groups, there are five orchestras, including the North Carolina Symphony based in Raleigh, and opera companies in Raleigh, Charlotte, Winston-Salem and Greensboro. The Frank Holder Dance Company also is in Greensboro, and the North Carolina Dance Theater, Winston-Salem, recently was accepted by its peers in London and New York City.

In crafts, in addition to Penland School and dozens of private studies, there is the John C. Campbell School, Brasstown, and two service organizations, the Piedmont Craftsmen and the Southern Highlands Handicraft Guild. The Arts Journal, published in Asheville, serves the state.

The outstanding gallery is the Southeastern Center of Contemporary Arts, Winston-Salem, which is in one of the Hanes' old houses. In one of the Reynolds' houses, Reynolda, is a beautiful collection of American Art. One of the Vanderbilt houses, Biltmore House, also is a museum, and that chateau is the centerpiece of a fabulous garden. Our great museum is the N.C. Museum of Art in Raleigh, the best in the region, and our best living museum is Old Salem, a restored Moravian town. Our best museum specializing in modern art, and that only, is the Witherspoon, Greensboro.

One year-round repertory company presently on the boards is the North Carolina Shakespeare Festival, High Point, which plays works of Shakespeare as well as others. Seasonal performances are given by many groups, and among outdoor dramas, we have "Unto These Hills" at Cherokee and "The Lost Colony" at Manteo. The Eastern Music Festival is held at Greensboro, the Brevard Music Center at Brevard. Among the most prestigious of all the summer performances are those at the American Dance Festival, Durham. The New Dance Company—a professional group—is located in Durham as well. The May Celebration of the Arts in Wilmington is a lively festival, with regional and national companies performing.

These organizations are independent of all others, each with its own board, its own funding, its own staff and professional direction. Except for one, the Witherspoon, they have grown up outside the universities, colleges and other sponsoring agencies. Professionalism has shouldered its way into the arts here; the artists have been made central to the arts, much as doctors are central to medicine. This seems to have encouraged, rather than discouraged, amateur companies.

And above, below, within and without all of these are the artists, our main treasure, who create art for us here and there as they choose. The other day I viewed four frescoes recently completed in rural churches near the mountain town of West Jefferson. Ben Long IV of Salisbury and Florence, Italy, did them. He used no organization at all, except the church's. On one occasion, he arrived with twenty helpers and went to work.

Artists do organize arts organizations, and so do patrons and other instigators and hangers-on-at-the-door. We need a variety of innovators, rich and poor, businessmen and music people. I recall happily many meetings over the years with any number of innovators: James Christian Pfohl, Robert Lee Humber, Vittorio Giannini, Ben Swalin, McNeil Lowry, Terry Sanford, Malcolm Morrison, Gordon Hanes, Robert Ward, James Semans, Mary Semans, Phil Hanes, Joan Hanes, Pete McKnight, Ted Potter, Phyllis Lang, Charlie Babcock, Barbara Millhouse, Earl Wynn, Zach Smith, Bill Brown, Bobby Lindgren, Leo Jenkins, Sam Ragan, Tom Kenan, Vicky Patton, Paul Green. Paul was a playwright, the writer of the "Lost Colony," founder of the outdoor drama movement and the Institute of Outdoor Drama, a poet who was active in support of the North Carolina Symphony, the Seagrove potters, and the School of the Arts when it was difficult to find many who favored it—as difficult as it is today to find any who do not. I can imagine Paul by the fire in his beautiful library, can almost hear his Harnett County rural accent, which he treasured. "The arts are the soul of a people," I hear him say, "their fire and spirit." He believed that, in those days, all seed cast in North Carolina fell on rocky ground. He planted art seed anyway, seeking ways to free the fire and spirit and to celebrate the dignity of the soul. He was an artist and that is an artist's work. It is the artist who can do that for us. That is what the best of this is all about.

Ever Friendly, Ever Vigilant

BY HUGH M. MORTON

The folks who know where it is happening in North Carolina, the ones who are concerned with income and employment, are believers in the "Big T's" — Textiles, Tobacco, and Travel & Tourism. These are the Tar Heel state's greatest providers, and of the three, Travel & Tourism may have the brightest future.

First of all, tasteful and prudent travel and tourism does not pollute or destroy. It can be replenished, to be used again and again. Its main asset, the varied natural beauty of North Carolina, with proper care will never become obsolete.

Perhaps most delightful of all, travel and tourism can and does flourish in many out-of-the-way rural counties that have little else to give their people income. It is the Number 1 employer in many of those areas.

It has long been the notion in defining industry that if it has a smokestack it is industry, if it doesn't it isn't. Travel and tourism, with its lack of smokestacks, is dissatisfied with that definition. As an industry it has had to scratch and claw for nearly all of its recognition and self-improvement that has occurred.

Thankfully, the State administration in recent years has been a friendly and understanding one toward travel and tourism. One illustration of this occurred when a former head of the Community College system was ready to scrap the all-important hospitality training program in the continuing education schools. The Governor personally stepped in to save the day. As a consequence hundreds of workers in restaurants, motels, resorts, and travel attractions have better jobs, and are performing more hospitably and efficiently in their careers.

Travel and tourism has jumped from around $1 billion in annual income to approaching $4 billion in the past few years, and I am one of many who has a hunch that even with those figures, the full story is not being told. For instance, when I pay carpenters to build condominiums at Grandfather Golf and Country Club, is that credited to travel and tourism? When Belk's in Charlotte sells a young lady a bikini to go to Lake Norman or the beach, is that classed as travel and tourism? I am reasonably certain that the answer is "no" in both instances, and that the true magnitude of travel and tourism in our state is not known or understood.

The travel industry recognizes probably better than any group the elements that are its strength. Good roads are absolutely essential, and as reluctant as we might have been to see additional taxes, travel leaders were at the forefront in passage of the additional gasoline taxes that were needed to keep North Carolina roads in suitable condition. Landmarks like historic Cape Hatteras Lighthouse must be preserved, and the Save Cape Hatteras

Hugh Morton is a photographer, writer and producer of award-winning films. He's also chairman of the Governor's Advisory Committee on Travel and Tourism, actively involved in the "Save the Cape Hatteras Lighthouse" movement and president of Grandfather Mountain. Morton won the North Carolina Award for Public Service in 1983.

Lighthouse Committee was set up as a subcommittee of the Travel Council of North Carolina. The Travel industry was also solidly behind the move to help protect the beauty of the mountains by enactment of the North Carolina Ridge Law.

One area of concern to me is the way that North Carolina goes about assessing its real estate taxes. I believe that environmentalists and others among us who are anxious to perpetuate the good life in the state have been quick to condemn the "evil" industrialists and developers, and slow to grasp the fact that zeal at the courthouse is nudging property owners into diminishing the amount of greenspace that they would otherwise prefer be left for people and wildlife to enjoy.

In my opinion, the man who owns pasture or woodland should be taxed for pasture and woodland, not for some inflated price that he might receive if he cut the land into lots or sold it to McDonald's for a fast food establishment. Land should be taxed for its current use, and the day its use changes,

the tax should change. That is fair, and it would certainly maintain North Carolina as the enjoyable place it is for a whole lot longer.

Economists forecast that between now and the year 2000 there will be a drop in industrial employment in North Carolina, and a rise in the service type jobs encompassed by the travel and tourism industry. What is already at least the No. 3 industry probably will advance to No. 2 with the millions of dollars that are being invested in expanded and improved travel facilities. We must be ever vigilant to keep North Carolina attractive, and I believe we will. Travel and tourism has a very bright future.

Research: Applying the Basics

BY GEORGE R. HERBERT

North Carolina's role in U.S. scientific research endeavors goes back many years before Research Triangle Institute was formed at the end of the 1950s to be the centerpiece for growth in the planned Research Triangle Park. North Carolinians at major university graduate schools, and in industrial laboratories, had come to prominence for their work in the agricultural sciences, textile and tobacco chemistry, statistics, medicine, sociology, and other disciplines. They were familiar names on national science boards, and as officers of leading professional societies.

Creation of the university-based Research Triangle Park, however, brought a totally new dimension to the state's place in the national scientific research community. Firms and agencies in the Park and at nearby universities and medical schools now employ dozens of the nation's top scientists in many fields. Their advances in basic and applied research, their new technology developments, and the new products and processes they create have gained recognition for North Carolina in the very front rank of national scientific achievement.

Formation of the Research Triangle Park and its subsequent growth have also had far-reaching implications for our state's economic well-being. It has sparked recent companion ventures such as the successful University Research Park in Charlotte, and the unprecedented Microelectronics Center of North Carolina. And it has been a key factor in attracting hundreds of millions of dollars of high technology investment throughout the state. Meanwhile, the Research Triangle itself has become one of North Carolina's most familiar place names to residents and outsiders alike.

States, cities, and university communities all across America are pinning their hopes for new investment, new employment, and

Herbert became the first employee and president of the Research Triangle Institute in late 1958. Prior to his North Carolina move, he served as executive associate director of Stanford University's Research Institute. A graduate of the U.S. Naval Academy, Herbert holds honorary degrees from The University of North Carolina at Chapel Hill, North Carolina State University and Duke University.

economic vitality on the ability to build research, development, and technology-based industrial activities. Virtually without exception, their model is North Carolina's Research Triangle Park.

Twenty-five years ago, that Park was an area of rolling hills and dry branch creeks, an area

populated mostly by possums and a few deer, and too poor for farming.

Today it is renowned as the largest planned scientific center in this country, and probably in the world. As former Governor Luther H. Hodges said, "There is nothing like it anywhere else, in fact, in spirit, or in purpose." Those three descriptors — fact, spirit, and purpose — tell a remarkable story, a story unique to North Carolina.

At mid-summer 1984, the facts are that the 5,800 acres of once empty pineland contain 47 industry, government, and university-related research facilities, and 56 support groups. Buildings and current construction projects have a brick and mortar value of more than $1.25 billion. Employment is nearly 25,000 and combined payrolls are $1 billion annually. All this on a previously unused and unpromising tract of real estate; no wonder North Carolina's Research Triangle Park is the envy of other states and regions.

Yet the Research Triangle Park did not happen easily, nor did it happen overnight.

That it exists at all is a tribute to the "spirit and purpose" of citizens throughout the state, and of the education, business, and government leaders who literally made it happen. They were convinced, and they backed their beliefs with time and effort, that building a science center here would create the new employment opportunities and attract the high technology industries that were bypassing North Carolina.

The principal asset fueling this conviction was the unique circumstance of three major research universities being clustered in a compact, triangle-shaped area near the center of the state. The University of North Carolina at Chapel Hill, Duke University in Durham, and North Carolina State University at Raleigh were recognized as the chief ingredients, and the starting place, for a sequence of education-research-industry enterprise that could help achieve the state's investment and employment goals.

Months of study concluded that such an undertaking was feasible, and at the end of December 1959 the nonprofit Research Triangle Foundation was formed for the sole purpose of promoting and developing a research park. Simultaneously, the separate, freestanding Research Triangle Institute was created by the universities to be the focal point for Park growth and to give initial evidence of activity there through the varied research services it provided under contract to industry and government clients.

Careful planning, enthusiastic university involvement, and strong leadership and commitment by the state's business and government communities have all combined through a quarter of a century to transform the Research Triangle dream into the glittering reality it is today.

Looking ahead, there is little doubt that North Carolina's industrial future is bright. That future will have been substantially influenced by the Research Triangle endeavor, by our universities, and by a spirit and purpose of cooperation between the educational enterprise, the corporate citizenry, and state government working together for the common good.

The Pursuit of Truth

BY FRYE GAILLARD

Though it seems hard to believe from the vantage point of today, the status of religion in North Carolina was a source of great concern in colonial times.

The colony was begun, in part, to spread the Christian gospel. But in 1717, Gov. Charles Eden wrote a letter to Anglican Church officials lamenting "the deplorable state of religion in this poor province." In 1739, Gov. Gabriel Johnston pointed out the "really scandalous" truth that religious services were regularly held in only two towns, Edenton and Bath.

By the latter part of the century, things had improved, but not enough to suit many church leaders. According to official estimates in 1790, only one North Carolinian in 30 was a member of a church (fewer than 14,000 out of a state population approaching 400,000). One Presbyterian minister, Eli Caruthers, declared that "men of education and especially the young men of the country thought it was a mark of independence to scoff at the Bible and professors of religion."

But in the 19th Century that picture began to change. With Baptists, Methodists and Presbyterians leading the way, a great religious awakening swept across the state. And as you sift through the dusty historical accounts of that awakening, one central idea begins to take shape: the pursuit of religious truth is a fractious undertaking, and most of the great currents that are present today — the doctrinal divisions and denominational competition, the zeal for evangelism and the pursuit of social justice — all have their antecedents in the mists of our history.

Today's "super churches," — for example, Charlotte's Northside Baptist with 6,000 members, or the Calvary Church across town where 3,700 people gather every Sunday — owe a certain debt of inspiration to Shubal

Gaillard is an editorial writer and former religion writer for the Charlotte Observer. He has written three books — *Watermelon Wine: The Spirit of Country Music; Race, Rock and Religion* and *The Catawba River.* Gaillard has been a journalist in North Carolina since 1972.

Stearns, a fiery Baptist minister from the 18th Century.

In 1755, the Rev. Stearns came to Guilford County and founded Sandy Creek Baptist, which was no different in scale than the largest churches of today. Originally, there were 16 members. Only a couple of years later, the membership had soared to 606 (37 times its

original size), and by the 1770s Sandy Creek had spawned 42 new churches and had sent forth 125 new ministers to preach the gospel.

During the next hundred years, the Baptists grew into the largest denomination in the state, and the descendents of the Sandy Creek congregation, known as the Separate Baptists, became the dominant faction. They split with the conservative, rigidly Calvinistic Primitive Baptists in 1830, and launched a progressive, evangelistic movement that soon led to the founding of Wake Forest College.

The split came after earnest, sometimes bitter disputes over the nature of religious truth, and the echoes of those disputes can still be heard. But the divisions were less important, finally, than the zeal to spread the word — an obsession that Baptists shared with their brethren in other denominations.

Indeed, North Carolina's spiritual ancestor to its native son, Billy Graham (who has preached to more people than any minister in history), was a circuit-riding Anglican by the name of John Boyd. In 1730, Boyd travelled 260 miles a month, mostly on horseback, but occasionally on foot, preaching and baptizing wherever crowds gathered. By the end of the year, he had converted more than 1,000 people.

A hundred years later, the most visible (and also the noisiest) form of evangelism in North Carolina was the Methodist camp meeting, where people assembled for a week at a time and powerful orators worked themselves and their followers into a jubilant frenzy. But the Methodists were known for something else as well. The most prophetic of them believed that Christianity has implications in the realm of human ethics, and they joined small, but tenacious factions of Moravians and Quakers in opposing the most controversial practice of the day: the institution of slavery.

The issue eventually split the Methodists, Baptists and Presbyterians into Northern and Southern branches, and most members of those denominations shared the prevailing local attitudes. But the dissenters were far more important than their numbers indicate. Like their counterparts who stood against segregation a hundred years later — large numbers of eloquent black ministers and a few stubborn whites ranging from Billy Graham to the more radical W. W. Finlator of Raleigh — they gave voice to a truth that later became reality.

Randolph Taylor, a Charlotte minister who, in 1983, led the successful national movement to reunify the Northern and Southern branches of the Presbyterian church, says religion is too important to be divorced from the realities of life. Church people, he added, "tend to be in positions of influence and decision-making. We can make a difference."

In North Carolina, they have for several centuries — not only in the pursuit of social justice, but in the promulgation of a message that offers people hope.

A Balanced Agriculture

BY DR. J. E. LEGATES

When our settlers took up holdings in North Carolina, nearly everyone was involved in farming, the production of food and fiber. Today, only about three percent of our state's citizens are so engaged. Yet agricultural production and productivity have grown tremendously. North Carolina is a strong agricultural state and a growing one. Since the 1950's, sales of products on farms have increased fourfold, to well over four billion dollars. The wide variety of products from

North Carolina farms generate a retail sales volume of over 20 billion.

A long held dream of the state's agricultural leaders is now becoming a reality. A balanced agriculture, the goal for several decades, is now on the horizon. Our state's varied soils and climate, plus a transportation system that capitalizes on its proximity to a large portion of our nation's population, has fostered this growth and development.

While tobacco is expected to continue to bring Tar Heel farmers a billion dollars annually, rapid advances in several commodities have been strikingly evident and will continue with proper market incentives. In the early 50's only about 20 percent of farm sales came from livestock and livestock products. Now in the early 80's, they account for over 40 percent of farm sales, that have in the meantime quadrupled.

Dramatic increases in poultry and swine production have elicited much national attention. Combined sales of broilers, eggs and turkeys now approach one billion dollars. Swine provide over $400 million to our pork producers. The burgeoning country ham industry, which now has a distinctive North Carolina flavor and reputation, has a $200 million sales volume.

Growth of the livestock and poultry

industry also has stimulated production of feed grains and forage crops. Corn and soybeans have become major enterprises, leaping over cotton and peanuts in acreage and value. Since the state continues to have a deficit of feed grains, there is further incentive to increase their production as transportation costs rise. More recently, vegetables, fruits, ornamentals, and flouriculture, including greenhouse production, have increased dramatically.

Nationally, North Carolina ranks first in farm receipts from farm forestry, sweet potatoes, tobacco and turkeys; second in processing cucumbers; fourth in broilers and eggs; and seventh in swine. Average milk production for our dairy cows on test is tops in the Southeast and in the top ten nationally. A new generation of aggressive, technically-trained, financially sensitive North Carolina farmers has become competitive with others in the U.S. in producing a diverse mix of quality crops and livestock.

It also has become evident that we can't just grow crops. We must have a substantial continuing market. For many new products such markets are extremely difficult to develop. This is especially true of our overseas markets. Yet our state ranks in the top ten for agricultural exports. Our port facilities, varied commodity mix and closeness to world centers of communication should enhance future exports that are much needed to keep our total economy strong.

As our capacity and capability to produce have moved forward, it has become clearly evident that we must process what we

Considered one of the country's leading authorities on animal genetics, Dr. Legates has won several prestigious awards for research in the field. He joined the faculty of North Carolina State University in 1949, and in 1971 was appointed Dean of the School of Agricultural and Life Sciences, the position he holds today.

produce. In this way we capitalize on the natural increase from our soil and climate in producing the product. Then we add further value to the product through processing and preservation. Finally we are in a position to share the additional value from retail sales of the finished product. We cannot permit our raw products to move to other states and lose these increments of added value, plus essential jobs for our citizens. Giant strides have been made to "process what we produce," and further efforts are bringing plants to our state to process our quality agricultural products.

North Carolina agriculture is adaptive, dynamic and varied. Its remarkable progress has been realized because of the strong cooperative and supportive linkages among the farm population, agribusiness, state government, and university personnel. Commodity and farm organizations have provided able leadership to foster programs for production and market development. Farmers themselves have directly provided funding beyond appropriations to support research and extension efforts. Too often these strong supportive relationships have been taken for granted since they have become traditional in North Carolina.

Our state's farmers can continue to provide the needed food and fiber to their fellow citizens with quality and abundance. Competent and trained personnel are active in the many segments of agricultural production, processing, marketing, and financing. Our record of growth and development has exceeded that of other sections of the nation, and we have tremendous untapped resources which can be used to an even greater advantage. Our future competitive position is strong.

125

An Educational Evolution

BY DR. A. CRAIG PHILLIPS

The history of public education in North Carolina shows the efforts made to fulfill the philosophy of educating every citizen. In the early 1900's, Governor Charles B. Aycock called for improving the system of education within the state, pleading for the right of every child born on earth to have the opportunity "to burgeon out all that there is within him."

Soon after the first Englishmen settled in North Carolina, missionaries of the Church of England arrived and attempted to establish a church and a school in every settlement. In addition to these early efforts by the church, public records show that the province also sought to aid education by providing for compulsory education of destitute orphans. In order to help these children become self-supporting, useful members of society, they were bound to someone who taught them a trade and also saw that they learned to read and write.

Legislation further provided for public education in the province. Several towns established schools, Edenton and New Bern being among the first. State funds aided the school at Edenton. New Bern's school, begun in 1766, was the first in the state to receive aid in the form of gifts of public land and annual public taxes. This marked the beginnings of our public school system of today, supported almost entirely by taxation and devoted to the education of all children in the state.

The State Constitution of 1776 encouraged the establishment of schools throughout the state to provide instruction at "low prices." Under this authority, numerous early schools and academies were chartered.

In 1817, Archibald D. Murphey reported to the General Assembly on education. Murphey, known as the "Father of the Common School," envisioned a state-operated public education program. He felt the future of North Carolina rested in the state's youth, recommending that regardless of class, educational opportunities be provided at public expense. Murphey's reports increased awareness of the need for a broad education system.

To financially aid the educational cause, North Carolina established a "Literary Fund" in 1825, made up of bank stocks, proceeds from sales of vacant lands, dividends from navigation companies, license taxes, and money received from the Federal Government for aid in the removal of the Cherokees. The proceeds from this endowment helped subsidize schools.

Finally, in January, 1839, the legislature passed the first common school law of North Carolina. This first law established the principle of combined State and local funds to provide for school support, a principle continued in all subsequent school legislation.

This first public school law had some weaknesses. Nothing was mentioned about providing schoolhouses or about employing teachers. Nor was mention made of subjects to be taught, or of a central authority at the head of the system of superintendent, committeemen, and teachers. And yet, in spite of these weaknesses, the public schools came to stay in North Carolina; the foundation of our present public school system was laid.

The period following the enactment of the first public school legislation found North Carolina making earnest, but floundering attempts to further establish its school system. Lack of organization and leadership caused this slow start. In 1852, the legislature created the office of Superintendent of Common Schools, and elected Calvin H. Wiley to fill this position. Under Wiley's leadership, the system steadily progressed. Improvements included organization of the system, better financial support, improved local management, better trained teachers, and a professional organization for teachers.

By the outbreak of war in 1860, North Carolina had developed one of the best educational systems in the South. However, this system did not remain untouched by the tragedies of war and the period of social, economic, and political confusion that followed. Some of the schools managed to

Dr. Phillips has been Superintendent of Public Instruction for the state since 1969. He has served in numerous state and national educational associations including membership, by presidential appointment, of the Inter-governmental Advisory Council of Education. A Greensboro native, Dr. Phillips received his own education at The University of North Carolina at Chapel Hill.

stay open during this period, but as banks failed, stocks depreciated, and school funds were swept away, the entire system suffered severely.

During the period following the War until about 1900, the school system had to be reconstructed. The Constitution of 1868 created the office of the Superintendent of Public Instruction to replace the old office of Superintendent of Common Schools, earlier abolished. The Legislature of 1869 reenacted practically the same legislation included in the law of 1839, adding a definitely prescribed school term, a general school tax, and a provision for the education of blacks. Poverty, inexperience, ignorance, prejudice, and the fear of mixed schools handicapped the reconstruction of the public school system in North Carolina. Rebuilding the school system was about as difficult as building it had been 30 years before. Despite the many obstacles, with the help of local legislation and private aid, the school system of the state once again showed signs of life. Many of the larger towns established free schools based on local taxation.

In 1875, the Reconstruction regime was overthrown, and the Constitutional Convention of that year planned for a new State law calling for separate schools for white and black children. County commissioners were charged with the financial responsibility for the maintenance and operation of the public schools and given taxing authority to support them.

Any townships with cities of more than 5,000 residents were authorized to establish separate school districts and support them through tax revenues. This led to the proliferation of city and county school systems across the state.

During the first quarter of the twentieth century, education progressed rapidly. Charles B. Aycock, governor of the state from 1901 to 1905, was very much aware of North Carolina's educational needs, and did much to bring them to the attention of the state's citizens. In 1901, the Literary Fund was reorganized, money being set aside as a revolving loan fund for building schoolhouses. Many new buildings were constructed, and old ones better equipped. The Legislature authorized counties to issue local bonds for school construction, and also authorized rural high schools.

In 1919, the minimum constitutional school term increased from four to six months. Legislation strengthened child labor laws and mandated compulsory school attendance for children ages eight through 12. Interest was raised for improving educational opportunities for blacks. Because of concern for teachers' qualifications, legislation passed to strengthen the state's teacher training institutions. Teachers' salaries increased, and school administration improved, stimulating the professional spirit of teachers. Informing the public about improvements in the school system helped make North Carolinians aware and proud of educational efforts in the state.

The third decade of this century is known as an Era of Prosperity for the state and the

nation. Agriculture and industry progressed rapidly as did other institutions. Education was one of these. Vocational education was introduced in the state's high schools. Legislation extended the school term to eight months, and the State assumed the responsibility for the school system's complete support. More and more children came to school on buses supported by public monies. During the Depression years, teachers' salaries and other educational expenses were reduced out of the need to cut State expenditures; however, educational progress continued. In 1935, a plan established state textbook rental and, the following year, provided free textbooks for elementary grades.

Improvements continued into the 1940's, and further changes occurred in the school system. Legislation provided a retirement plan for State employees, including all public school personnel. Further changes increased the compulsory attendance age from 14 to 16, added the twelfth grade, extended the school term to nine months, and created the school lunch program.

During the second half of this century, the Civil Rights Movement affected North Carolina's school system. In 1954, the U.S. Supreme Court ruled against separation of races in public schools in Brown vs Board of Education of Topeka. The following year, the North Carolina General Assembly passed the Pearsall Plan, a bill transferring the complete authority over enrollment and assignment of children in public schools and buses from the State Board of Education to county and city boards. In 1964, the national Civil Rights Act was passed; discrimination in public education was prohibited.

Other changes occurred in North Carolina's school system during the second half of this century. In the sixties, North Carolina implemented an experimental state-wide program, the Comprehensive School Improvement Project aimed at improving instruction at the primary level, with particular emphasis on language arts and arithmetic. The State included high schools in the free textbook program. Beginning in 1965 with the Elementary and Secondary Education Act, about 12 to 15 percent of the funding for public schools came from the Federal Government. This act included funds for the disadvantaged and handicapped, as well as funds for libraries and experimental programs. In 1969, North Carolina first expended tax money for kindergarten education, and two years later, the Legislature approved a state-wide kindergarten program.

In 1971, a North Carolina Constitutional revision made the State Superintendent the secretary and chief administrative officer of the State Board of Education. The constitutional changes created the State Department of Public Education composed of the State Department of Public Instruction, Department of Community Colleges, and the Controller's Office of the State Board of Education. Continued efforts to improve the educational system included the establishment of eight Regional Centers throughout the state, and the extension of the teachers' school term to ten months to allow time for planning and in-service training. By 1976-77, the kindergarten program was available to all children in the state.

One of the state's most notable contributions to education was the North Carolina School of the Arts, which was established in 1963 in Winston-Salem for high school and college students preparing for professional careers in the arts. The North Carolina School of Science and Mathematics opened in 1980 in Durham as a public boarding school for high school students with strong aptitudes in science and math. The State pays tuition, room and board in order not to exclude any deserving student.

Higher education in North Carolina has also long been a major recipient of State support. From the founding of the University of North Carolina in 1789 in Chapel Hill, the State's institutions of higher education have served as models for the systems in other states. Today the system boasts 16 campuses across the state, including UNC in Chapel Hill and N.C. State University in Raleigh. Duke University in Durham is the largest of more than 40 private colleges and universities across the state.

In 1981, a separate state board was established for community colleges, and there are currently 58 community colleges and technical institutes across the state.

In April 1984, the North Carolina Commission on Education for Economic Growth completed an extensive study of the State's public schools and proposed specific recommendations to meet the challenge of providing students with the skills needed for the future. These include setting up task forces in local communities on education for economic growth, promoting students only when they have mastered required competencies, raising pay for teachers and administrators, reducing class size, and continuing to serve students with exceptional needs.

The State continues to show concern for seeing that each child in the state receives the best possible education. Annual testing is being used to diagnose individual learning needs in grades 1, 3, 6, and 9, and in the eleventh grade, competency testing is being used to make sure high school graduates have the knowledge and skills to cope with everyday living.

Many changes occurred in North Carolina's educational system as it evolved. The success of North Carolina's public school system through financial panics and wars is the greatest single service the State has rendered its citizens.

Politics and Paradox

BY ROY PARKER, JR.

North Carolina has a politics consistent with its varied landscape. It is a politics of sharp contrasts, as rich as the differences between a Smoky Mountains cove and the crash of surf on a Hatteras beach.

This variety in the public life of the state challenges commentators to define it, and produces such paradoxical perspectives as that of the political scientist who concluded it was a "progressive plutocracy."

In its earlier history, North Carolina politics was often the butt of ridicule. A colonial visitor from Virginia christened it "Lubberland." Another, writing about turmoil over colonial policies, lamented, "Poor Carolana!" And in the early 19th century, North Carolinians referred to themselves as "The Rip Van Winkle State." Contrasted to proud Virginia on the north and proud South Carolina to the south, North Carolina seemed even to revel in the saying that it was "a vale of humility between two mountains of conceit!"

The political personalities of the state were epitomized by Congressman Nathanial Macon, whose frugality and zeal for states rights made his name synonymous with the staunch conservatism which has been an enduring element of North Carolina politics. He even objected to an appropriation for a mausoleum for George Washington, calling it a wicked fruit of "this monument mania."

While Macon was the example of parsimonious rectitude, Congressman Duncan McFarland of the Fayetteville District represented the rambunctious, even riotious tradition. He had fist fights, was convicted of rape, charged with Toryism, murder, perjury, hog-stealing, forgery, and witchcraft. He was rotten-egged in the campaign of 1804, yet the voters liked him enough to elect him to six terms in the General Assembly and one in Washington.

These elements of politics contrasted with a more progressive, visionary, and sober side to public life in North Carolina.

Leaders like William R. Davie and Archibald Debow Murphey took the lead in

Journalism is his vocation, history his avocation. Once Washington correspondent for The News and Observer, Parker was the founding editor of The Fayetteville Times, a position he still holds. He is a member of the board of the North Carolina Literary and Historical Association and the North Carolina Arts Council.

establishing the University of North Carolina and launching a widespread program of "internal improvements," roads, bridges, canals, railroads, and waterways. Government began to serve the people with passage in 1839 of a statewide education law and in 1848 of a law establishing a state institution for the insane. In all of these things, North Carolina government was actually in the vanguard at least among southern states.

The Civil War produced more paradox. More young men from North Carolina died for the Confederacy than from any other state. Yet Governor Zeb Vance and a sizeable portion of the state's population were either constantly critical or openly defiant of the southern states government and its aims.

And so this paradox lives on today.

North Carolina's politics runs the gamut from arch conservative to proud liberal. There are sharp differences along political party lines. There are regional differences and racial differences, rural-versus-urban differences, even age and sex differences. Political campaigns have become big business in the state, costing millions of dollars, reflecting in part the need to appeal to so diverse an electorate. The diversity is reflected, too, in the people who hold elective office in North Carolina. They span the ideological spectrum.

The tradition of progressive state and local government has been an enduring one. North Carolina's powerful General Assembly, which is unfettered by gubernatorial veto, has cooperated with forward-looking governors and together they have made the state a leader in highways, medical care, environmental protection, and above all, in higher education and public schooling.

The inherent conservatism has been cast aside at times, especially in the name of culture, as North Carolina provided public dollars to establish a state art museum and a state school for performing artists. As early as the 1920s, the state contracted with the famed Brookings Institution to bring businesslike organization and procedures to its budget-making, resulting in an appropriations process which has been remarkably free from scandal if not from the usual political log-rolling. After World War II, the same sort of modernization was applied to the state's judicial system, and both its courts and its statute books were shaped to make justice more evenhanded and effective. The organizational structure of the executive branch was modernized a decade ago, and North Carolina county and municipal governments were provided with adequate powers to carry out a widening array of public services and initiatives at the grassroots level.

In these times as in times past, North Carolina strives to live up to a motto coined in the ancient times of Rome and adopted 90 years ago, "to be, rather than to seem." Out of this striving comes the diversity of its public life, its politics of paradoxes and its government of generous goals. North Carolina continues to be an exciting commonwealth with a future of hopeful progress for all its people.

The Economic Edge

BY IVIE L. CLAYTON

Historically, the economy in North Carolina has lagged behind the nation. But over the past two decades, the state has experienced rapid growth. Through the year 2000, economic growth in North Carolina is expected to continue to outperform the nation.

Between 1960 and 1980, personal income in North Carolina grew by 140 percent (even after accounting for inflation.) North Carolina edged closer to U.S. per capita income, up from 71 percent in 1960 to 84 percent in 1980.

The mix of manufacturing jobs has been changing in North Carolina. Some of the new, higher wage industries such as high-technology, rubber and chemicals have been growing very rapidly, while more traditional industries such as textiles have shown a decline in employment.

R. J. Reynolds Industries, headquartered in Winston-Salem, continues to be North Carolina's largest company followed by Burlington Industries and Blue Bell, Inc. The three largest privately-held companies in the state are McDevitt and Street Co., MacField Texturing, and Dillard Paper Co.

In 1980, the value of shipments abroad approached $4 billion. Thirty percent of agricultural produce and six percent of manufacturing output was sold on the international market.

Agriculture, forestry, and seafood will continue to play a key role in the North Carolina economy, especially as international demand for these products continues to grow. North Carolina anticipates a decline in dependence on tobacco as a major cash crop. Cultivation of fruits and vegetables offers an alternative to tobacco, but requires large amounts of water and capital.

North Carolina's heritage of clean air, productive lands, and abundant water has contributed to the high quality of life. However, as economic and industrial growth continues, the potential clash with environmental concerns increases.

As an example of the attention being given to these concerns, the General Assembly in

Clayton is president of the North Carolina Citizens for Business and Industry, based in Raleigh. A former Commissioner of the North Carolina Department of Revenue, he is a past president of the National Association of Tax Administrators. Clayton is a native of Roxboro and an opera fan.

June 1984 established a Hazardous Waste Treatment Commission to identify a suitable site for the location of a hazardous waste treatment facility. Besides having the authority to condemn property, the commission can recommend that the Governor's Waste Management Board override local ordinances.

A large share of the state's population lives in areas which are expected to have

insufficient water in the future. Three of the state's four major river basins are already approaching the limits of supply in their upper reaches. They are also the basins for which major growth is projected. Water is likely to become one of the major considerations in economic development during the next two decades, particularly in the Piedmont Crescent cities of Charlotte, Winston-Salem, Greensboro, Durham and Raleigh.

With increased population in North Carolina, more land will be needed for residential, commercial, and industrial development. Much of this land will come from farm and woodlands. If current trends continue, nearly 700,000 acres of prime farmland will be lost to development by 2000.

North Carolina is uniquely situated to place equal emphasis on both new and traditional industries, thereby avoiding the massive financial outlays and extensive dislocation generally associated with radical changes in an industrial base. North Carolina's traditional industries — agriculture, textiles, apparel and furniture — are already undergoing significant changes in their efforts to survive the economic recession and regain their position in international markets.

These industries long served as the backbone for employment in North Carolina, are still viable and remain the state's leading sources of employment. The challenge is to encourage the appropriate use of technical advances and organizational innovations to maintain the state's base in traditional industries.

In North Carolina, the choice is not between high-technology industry and traditional industries. Instead, the focus of policymaking is on how best to strengthen the existing industrial base while enhancing that base with fast-growing, high-technology companies.

As early as 1956, then Governor Luther Hodges met with representatives from the three leading Triangle universities — the University of North Carolina at Chapel Hill, North Carolina State University in Raleigh and Duke University in Durham — and members of the local business community to discuss the concept of a research park.

The Research Triangle Park actually became a reality in the mid-1960s, when IBM Corporation and a major research and administrative complex of the U.S. Environmental Protection Agency (EPA) located there. Encouraged by the Park's success, economic development efforts in North Carolina have focused on the recruitment of high-technology firms, particularly over the past six years.

Under the leadership of Governor James B. Hunt, Jr., the state's economic development strategy has also included direct state funding for high-technology centers, such as the Microelectronics Center of North Carolina and the North Carolina Biotechnology Center (both based in the Research Triangle Park).

Efforts to strengthen and upgrade mathematics and science education in the state's elementary and secondary schools are also considered important components of an overall economic development strategy. The North Carolina School of Science and Mathematics was established by the 1978 General Assembly as the first in the nation and as an example of a new initiative in education.

Another major legislative action affecting business was approved by the 1984 General Assembly when the bill was enacted to authorize North Carolina bank holding companies to acquire or merge with banks in 13 other southern states.

The transition from a traditional economy based on agriculture and manufacturing in textiles and furniture to a new economy characterized by a growing service sector and advanced-technology industries has only begun in North Carolina.

The recruitment of manufacturing firms is the primary function of the N. C. Department of Commerce. The department often takes the lead in efforts to attract new plants to the state, and at other times the department assists

the efforts of local development corporations, Chambers of Commerce and other community organizations.

The list of manufacturing firms attracted to the state since 1983 alone is impressive and includes the following firms with over $10 million each in investments: AGA Gas in Wake Forest, Bendix Corporation in Rocky Mount, Glaxo, Inc. in Zebulon, Lutravil Company in Durham, Owens-Illinois, Inc. in Hamlet, Square D Company in Monroe, Takeda Chemical Industries in the Wilmington area, Toleram Fibers, Inc. in Ansonville, Dow Jones, Inc. (The Wall Street Journal) in Charlotte, Outboard Marine Corporation in Burnsville and American Honda Motor Company near Mebane.

Recruitment successes over the past year also include firms largely engaged in research and development activities: division headquarters for General Electric/Intersil Semiconductor; headquarters for ITT Corporation's North America telecommunications products business; and headquarters for the Semiconductor Research Corporation.

New and expanded plants announced for North Carolina during the first half of 1984 totaled $1.3 billion for a projected increase of 27,000 jobs. This compares with $918 million and 10,762 jobs for the first six months of 1983. The previous record investment of $1.1 billion was announced during the first six months of 1981.

Major announcements included a $100 million plant for Kimberly-Clark in Lexington, RCA Corp. in Weaverville, an expansion of Northern Telecom, Inc. in Research Triangle Park, Wang Laboratories, Inc. in Asheville, Semicon, Inc. in Woodland and Channelmaster in Smithfield.

North Carolina Citizens for Business and Industry, chartered as the North Carolina Citizens Association in 1942, has worked with government on all levels to help create a favorable business climate in North Carolina.

It was created by North Carolina business leaders who understood the vital necessity to maintain and expand policies that would allow business to operate in an environment where the tax burden is fair and competitive with neighboring states, government regulations few and reasonable, employer-employee relationships harmonious, and the relationship between business and government both friendly and cooperative.

By 1984, 42 years after is formation, Citizens for Business and Industry has grown tremendously in the size of its membership and staff, and in the scope of its operations. But the goal is still to preserve and improve even further North Carolina's deserved reputation as an ideal home for any business of any size or type.

A nonprofit, nonpartisan corporation, composed of more than 1,650 business members, the organization includes both large multinational corporations in the Fortune 500 listings and businesses of modest size with only a few employees. The Raleigh-based staff numbers 12 people, including the president and staff director. Four other officers, an executive committee and a 100-member board of directors guide the affairs of the organization.

North Carolina has a population of about six million people, continues to grow faster than the national average, and continues to improve the personal income of its citizens. North Carolina's population will increase by 30 percent or almost two million people between 1980 and 2000. While this growth is substantial, it is less rapid than the growth experienced between 1960 and 1980.

If current trends continue, 1.1 million households will be added between 1980 and 2000. This represents an increase of 50 percent, while population is expected to grow by only 30 percent during this same period.

But what really makes North Carolina is its quality of life. What other State has as many advantages as North Carolina? It is a state with a great art Museum, a fine University system, and tremendous natural beauty. The challenge for North Carolina's next 400 years is to preserve these advantages and build on them.

The "Writingest" State

BY DORIS BETTS

William Shakespeare was 24 and had not yet produced a play when the first book about North Carolina was published in England in 1588, a 48-page account of a year his contemporary, Thomas Hariot, had spent with Sir Walter Raleigh's first colony on Roanoke Island.

Since then, volumes by or about Tar Heels have kept catalogers busy at the North Carolina Library in Raleigh, Duke's Southern Collection, the North Carolina Collection at the University of North Carolina at Chapel Hill and elsewhere, while Professor Richard Walser, North Carolina State University, has proved the state's most devoted and prolific literary historian.

Many kinds of North Carolina novels have been written since Virginia native Robert Strange, a lawyer and U.S. Senator living in Fayetteville, published the state's first novel, *Eonegusky* (1839), with themes echoing James Fenimore Cooper's about a friendly Cherokee chief fighting with Andrew Jackson and the pioneers against Creek Indians. The first novelist actually born here, Calvin Wiley, was also North Carolina's first superintendent of

common schools. He published *Alamance* (1847) and *Roanoke* (1849).

From that time, novels have flowed from pens, clacked off typewriters and been screened by word processors.

Until her death in 1920, Christian Reid, Salisbury, wrote as "Frances Fisher" 46 books of the southern foothills. Thomas Dixon, Shelby, is remembered for *The Leopard's Spots* (1902) and *The Clansman* (1905), which became the classic film, *The Birth of a Nation*. Olive Tilford Dargan's novels include *Call Home the Heart* (1932) about the Gastonia strikes. Inglis Fletcher, Edenton, covered the state in 12 historical novels, among them *The Scotswoman* (1955) about Flora MacDonald. After Mississippian James Boyd moved to Southern Pines in 1919, he produced several novels about his adopted state, *Marching On* (1927) and *Long Hunt* (1930). His home, Weymouth, is now preserved for use as a writers' colony.

The first novel about North Carolina people to win a national award was *Purslane* (1939) by Bernice Kelly Harris, who wrote six others set in Wake and Northampton counties. In Huntersville, Legette Blythe has produced 24 books, both novels and non-fiction. Another prolific author, Manley Wade Wellman, since 1951 in Chapel Hill has produced many adventure stories, some set here during the Revolutionary War, others Appalachian mysteries for boys.

Some write for the young, but others teach them directly. No survey of the state's literature should underestimate the influence of North Carolina's remarkable teachers of writing.

Phyllis Peacock of the Raleigh schools typifies hundreds of unsung heroic English teachers in Tar Heel high schools who have encouraged talent.

And Betty Smith, for example, was one of many drawn to Chapel Hill by the playwriting courses of Professor Frederick H. Koch, who began teaching there in 1918 and nurtured generations of writers until his death in 1944. Smith's *A Tree Grows in Brooklyn* became an all-time best seller, a film and a Broadway musical. Another Koch student, Frances Gray Patton, Durham, wrote the popular *Good Morning, Miss Dove* and published many deft stories in *The New Yorker*. And one of Prof. Koch's most successful graduates was Thomas Wolfe, Asheville, whose *Look Homeward, Angel* has cast here in North Carolina as long a shadow as the works of Faulkner have cast in Mississippi.

LITERATURE

Phillips Russell, whose novel *Fumbler* is less well known than his many biographies, drew many students, as did Jessie Rehder (*Remembrance Way*). Novelist and story writer Max Steele, whose *Debby* won the Harper novel prize, has succeeded them and heads the writing program at Chapel Hill. At Duke, William Blackburn taught Anne Tyler, formerly of Raleigh whose early novels are set in North Carolina, as well as William Styron, Mac Hyman and two Tar Heel novelists who have themselves become influential teachers: Reynolds Price and Fred Chappell. Price, now at Duke, won the Faulkner award for *A Long and Happy Life* (1962); Canton native Fred Chappell, now a professor at the University of North Carolina at Greensboro (which has the state's only M.F.A. program in writing) creates dense psychological novels like *Dagon* and *The Gaudy Place*.

Poet Randall Jarrell, whose *Pictures From an Institution* satirized academia, taught Sylvia Wilkinson, who has written novels of growing up in Durham County or murder in Madison County (*Shadow of the Mountain*, 1977).

Another Jarrell student, Heather Ross Miller, sets her novels in her native Stanly County (*Gone a Hundred Miles*, 1966) and teaches at Pfeiffer College. And Sam Ragan at N.C. State and Sandhills College has taught many writers.

Former New York editor Guy Owen worked with poets and fiction writers at N.C. State; his comic novel, *Ballad of the Flim-Flam Man,* and its subsequent film depicted the Cape Fear Basin, while *Journey for Joedel* (1970) about an Indian boy was a Pulitzer nominee. Lee Smith, who teaches at N.C. State, and John Barth were fortunate to have been students of Louis Rubin, another novelist-teacher at Chapel Hill. John Foster West (*Time Was*) teaches writing at Appalachian; Maya Angelou (*I Know Why the Caged Bird Sings*) is at Wake Forest; and Ovid Williams Pierce, whose books concentrate on what happened to plantation life after the Civil War, is at East Carolina. Peggy Hoffman, in Raleigh since 1950, wrote *A Forest of Feathers* based on experiences at Butner, but much of her fiction has international sources. So do the dozen books of Robert Ruark, Southport, although *The Old Man and the Boy* (1957) is a memoir of life with his grandfather.

Asheville native Wilma Dykeman has often depicted the tough, independent people of the mountains; *The Tall Woman* (1966) continues to attract young, feminist readers. Another Asheville native, John Ehle, has set his many novels in every region of the state as well as Europe; *The Land Breakers* (1964) and *The Road* (1967) focus on mountain people. During the 1960s, as advisor to Gov. Terry Sanford, Ehle initiated new programs in education and the arts that continue to provide the reality behind the bumper-sticker slogan: NORTH CAROLINA: THE STATE OF THE ARTS.

Journalist and commentator Tom Wicker, Hamlet, has written seven novels, some under a pen name, including *The Kingpin* (1963). Daphne Athas teaches at Chapel Hill, the setting for Entering Ephesus (1971). Ben Haas, Raleigh, published under various names, but *Look Away, Look Away* (1964) with its racial themes and *The Chandler Heritage* (1972) about cotton mills and their owners brought his widest audiences. Mississippian James Street spent the last nine years of his life in the Tar Heel state, continuing his long string of historical novels, such as *Tap Roots* and *The Velvet Doublet.*

Space will not permit discussion of the state's many prominent novelists. The North Carolina Writers' Conference has over 200 members, and the national directory, *Poets and Writers,* names 98 Tar Heels with recent work in print. I even write a little fiction myself!

Other fiction forms include the short story and theater. William Sydney Porter, Greensboro, is well known for his short stories published under the name O. Henry. Others known for their work in this form: Wilbur Daniel Steele, Richard Chase, Charles Edward Eaton, Marianne Gingher, Larry

Doris Betts is Alumni Distinguished Professor of English and chairs the faculty at The University of North Carolina at Chapel Hill. As one of the state's most prominent writers, she has received the Sir Walter Raleigh Award on three occasions; in 1975, the North Carolina Legislature presented her with the North Carolina Award and Medal for Literature. Betts started her career as a newspaperwoman.

Ruderman, Ruth Moose, Joe Ashby Porter, Hoke Norris, Shirley Cochrane, Hallie Burnett and others.

In 1759, Thomas Godfrey, Jr., Wilmington, wrote and produced *The Prince of Parthia,* five acts in blank verse, the first American tragedy. Edward Hall and Lemuel Sawyer were other playwrights of the last century.

In this century, the arrival of Frederick Koch from North Dakota to start the Carolina Playmakers and encourage the use of local talent stimulated many writers. His best-known drama student is Paul Greene, founder of the outdoor drama. Green, from Lillington, won in 1927 the Pulitzer Prize for *In Abraham's Bosom,* but he is best remembered for the first of his four outdoor symphonic dramas, *The Lost Colony,* which has been running on Roanoke Island in the summers since 1937.

The western counterparts were outdoor dramas written by Kermit Hunter, *Unto These Hills* at Cherokee and *Horn in the West* at Boone. Other dramatists have included William and Martha Hardy, Samm Art Williams, James Reston, James Wall and Bland Simpson.

At the National Endowment for the Arts in 1980, I was told that the three busiest "writingest" states were New York, California and North Carolina.

Thus, if the Chinese proverb is correct — that a book is "like a garden carried in the pocket," — Tar Heels should have intellectually those "sweet and odoriferous flowers" as well as "faire fields and plains" which Verrazzano found here and wrote about in 1524. To a student of North Carolina writing, there seems an endless garden of both fiction and the second crowded prose category, non-fiction, which stretches from scholarship to cookbooks. Again, space does not permit even a sampling of North Carolina's prominent authors in the various forms of non-fiction, but suffice it to say that North Carolinians have been and will continue to be well-remembered for their many contributions to literature in all its forms.

Living the Good Life in the Old North State

CHAPTER 5

No state surpasses North Carolina in the variety of its gems. Or their worth. The "Carolina Emerald," found near Statesville, for instance, was deemed by Tiffany and Company to be the largest and finest cut emerald on the continent. The green sparkler

Andy Griffith

was cut to 13 carats and valued at $100,000.

Yet, the state's most precious jewels are, and have always been, its people. And they are, on the whole, either unpolished or unpretentious — from Zeb Vance to Andy Griffith.

Carolinians have always taken the state's motto — "To Be Rather Than To Seem" as a credo. Any Tar Heel can give hundreds of examples. I recall the return of Vermont Royster to his home state a few years back to testify at a commission meeting. Mr. Royster was a world-renowned journalist and editor of "The Wall Street Journal."

When asked to introduce himself, he replied: "I am a Tar Heel by birth and a journalist by trade."

Sam J. Ervin Jr., the U.S. Senator from North Carolina who headed the committee which investigated Watergate, always referred to himself as "a country lawyer," despite a Harvard Law School degree.

Which doesn't mean that Carolinians aren't proud. Senator Sam once described himself, modestly, as a country lawyer to President Lyndon Johnson. Johnson laughed.

"Whenever I see a country lawyer approaching, I grab my pocketbook and run," the president retorted.

Chortling, the senator replied: "That's not surprising. Country lawyers often compel evildoers to disgorge their ill-gotten gains."

The state's people are so modest that hardly anyone knows North Carolina is a megastate.

The vale of humility between two

Sam J. Ervin Jr.

mountains of conceit (South Carolina and Virginia) has slipped past Massachusetts to become the nation's 10th most populous state, with over six million inhabitants.

Yet, it remains a modest megastate, confounding the urban experts, including Neal Peirce, the co-author of "The Book of America: Inside the Fifty States Today."

"It's a state which managed to industrialize without urbanizing," Peirce said, "so that it is still a very rural state."

Living close to the land has given the natives a fierce streak of independence. Every schoolboy knows that North Carolina was the next to the last state to ratify the U.S.

Constitution because the state's signers feared a central government which would be too strong. They signed once the Bill of Rights was added to protect the people.

That is the spirit, too, of the now legendary oysterman on Ocracoke who refused to put the large oysters on the top of his basket but always placed them on the bottom. It was, he said, "the only 'fahr' thing to do."

The independent thinking also produces anomolies in politics to this day. The same state that produced people like Luther Hodges, Terry Sanford and Jim Hunt has elected bedrock conservatives Jeese Helms and John East.

Yet, neither politics nor bad weather can separate Carolinians from their deep affection for their state or their neighbors.

Men and women whose politics are as different as the basketball styles of Wake Forest's Tyrone Bogues and UNC's Michael Jordan break cornbread together at church suppers and remain the best of friends.

The neighborliness extends to anyone who is a Tar Heel. In a state without a huge city there are hundreds of small towns. And each resident of a small town seems to know at least two or three people in other small towns as friends. This produces a bond of fellowship that stretches across the hamlets, crossroads and towns of North Carolina like an invisible web, for no one really meets a total stranger: "Oh, 'yew' all are from Kinston. Do you know the . . . . who live there?" The odds are

two to one that the stranger does know the Joneses, Smiths, or whoever, or their cousins. That's the way it is in North Carolina. And nobody wants to change it.

Terry Sanford

From the marsh grass on the coast to the moon-haunted pines on the slopes of the Smokies, Carolinians slog through life with a feeling of fellowship for other Tar Heels and a love of the land that gave them birth.

Maybe it is the land that gives them their independence. The land that the Gargantua of American letters, Thomas Wolfe of Asheville, described as: ". . . the place of autumnal moons hung low and orange at the frosty edges of the pines; it is the place of frost and silence; of the clean dry shocks and the opulence of enormous pumpkins that yellow on hard clotted earth; it is the place of the stir and feathery stumble of the hens upon their roost, the frosty, broken barking of the dogs, the great barnshapes and solid shadows in the running sweep of the moon-whited countryside . . ."

141

It is the big cash crop of the Tar Heel State. Over 450,000 short tons of tobacco are harvested each year, making the state the country's leading supplier.

The growing season for the leaf is short. So, the tobacco farmer is a busy man: weeding, fighting black shank and black root rot, topping the plant when it produces flowers so that the remaining leaves are larger and heavier.

The sweet and heady odor of tobacco curing to a low fire, the laughter and sweaty weariness as families tie the leaves for hanging, and the rhythmic chants of auctioneers in hundreds of tobacco warehouses down east are familiar and treasured experiences.

Perhaps the first North Carolinians out of bed each morning are its fishermen. At first light, they can be seen hauling lines on a trawler or wiping the sleep from their eyes on sandy beaches from Corolla to Calabash.

Commercial fishing is big business in the state, with annual catches valued at about $70 million. In good years, 150 million pounds of menhaden are caught by state fishermen. The fish is used for fertilizer and as an oil base for paint. Croaker, flounder, river-herring, striped bass and gray trout are the edible fish caught in greatest numbers.

"Early to bed, early to rise, fish like hell, make up lies," is the motto for both residents and visitors to the coast. Yet, when the channel bass or bluefish are running, there is a temptation to linger until the moon is up and thermos coffee is cold.

There are eight of the century-old lighthouses on the 301 miles of North Carolina shoreline, and each, like a great lady, has its own personality and manner of dress.

Perhaps the most charming is the squat, oystershell-white Ocracoke Lighthouse (at right). It is 76 feet tall, flashing a light visible for 14 miles. Built in 1823, the lighthouse at Ocracoke is one of the nation's oldest.

Taller and more imposing is the Bodie Island Lighthouse (above, left), near Oregon Inlet and the Herbert C. Bonner Bridge. Built in 1872, the distinctive black and white stripes encircle a structure that is 163 feet high. It projects a beam visible for 19 miles.

The Currituck Beach Lighthouse (above, center) at Corolla is one of the few lighthouses in the nation, and the only one of its type in the state, with an unpainted red brick exterior. Located halfway between Cape Henry and Bodie Island, it was built in 1895 and towers over 150 feet above the Atlantic.

Patterned after the French Chateau de Blois in the valley of the Loire River, the Biltmore House in Asheville (at left), created by George W. Vanderbilt in the early French renaissance style of Francis I, is one of the state's most famous tourist attractions. Begun in 1890, the chateau of Indiana limestone occupied an army of workmen for five years.

One of the noblest residences in the United States, the house itself is 780 feet long and occupies four acres. It contains a library housing 23,000 volumes, 40 master bedrooms and a huge medieval banquet hall. Biltmore brims with art treasures that Vanderbilt gathered from around the world.

More comfortable than Biltmore, though less pretentious, is the 102-year-old Green Park Inn (at right), perched 4,000 feet high in the Blue Ridge Mountains. Located at Blowing Rock, the inn is distinctive in that it literally straddles the Continental Divide. Allen and Pat McCain, the current owners, keep the inn open year-round, providing blankets for guests on summer nights when the rest of the state is sweltering in a heat wave.

Nowhere does the state's colonial heritage seem more evident than in Edenton, known as the "cradle of the colony." The oldest house in North Carolina — "Sycamore," built in 1660 near the Albemarle Sound — is found here. Named for the state's first governor, Charles Eden, it is a town of firsts. Here, too, is the home of Penelope Barker (at right), who presided over the first organized political activity by women in the colonies. In 1774, the women held the celebrated "Edenton Tea Party," at which they drank not tea but a concoction of boiled leaves to protest the tea tax levied by England.

The colonial heritage is evident today in Winston-Salem as well. Visitors to Old Salem will find homes of the pre-Revolutionary period and ladies wearing attire popular in the 1760s, as pictured at left. The city was founded in 1766 by members of the Moravian Church. Early craftsmanship still lingers in the hands of a woman in period costume who weaves a basket.

Echoes of struggle and achievement resound in ears attuned to history. Restored Fort Macon, at Atlantic Beach near Morehead City, is the site of Civil War reenactments punctuated with booming cannon, as depicted at left. Completed in 1834, the fort, built as part of a national system of maritime defenses, is an outstanding example of 19th century military architecture. It has a pentagonal court and is completely surrounded by a deep moat that is 25 feet wide. Named for U.S. Senator Nathaniel Macon, the fort was seized by North Carolina troops at the outbreak of the Civil War and surrendered, after a heavy bombardment, in 1862.

The hiss and puff of a steam locomotive can still be heard along a three-mile track in the high country of North Carolina where hundreds of thousands gather each year to ride the popular Tweetsie Railroad (at right). Originally used as a commercial railroad between Boone and Johnson City, Tennessee, the sightseeing train is the main attraction at The Tweetsie Railroad theme park, which opened to the public in 1956.

The home of Civil War Governor Zebulon Vance has been restored at Weaverville in the Reem's Creek Valley. A museum containing Vance memorabilia is adjacent to the five-room log cabin (above right) where Vance, who later became a U.S. Senator, was born.

The old and new in industry are brought into focus in these photographs of an old grist mill bearded with ice and a sun-soaked high-tech building at the Research Triangle Park between Raleigh and Durham.

The mill, located on Yates Pond in Wake County, is the oldest known mill still standing in that county. It was built between 1835 and 1840 on the original stone foundation dating back to the 1750s. Mills like this were used by the earliest settlers to grind corn.

The newer building is the corporate headquarters in the United States of the international Burroughs Wellcome Co., a world leader in the manufacture of pharmaceutical products. An architectural triumph with its open spaces and skylights, the building contains corporate offices and a laboratory in its 450,000 square feet of space. The structure was designed by award-winning architect Paul Rudolph, whose achievements include the Yale University School of Architecture building.

The state capitol (below), a masterpiece of Greek revival architecture, was begun in 1833 and constructed of locally quarried granite. Its distinctive rotunda is graced with a duplicate statue of George Washington by Antonio Canova (at left). The original statue was severely damaged in the fire of 1831 that destroyed the state house, which the present building replaced.

The executive mansion at 200 N. Blount Street in Raleigh stands on Burke Square (at right). The Queen Anne-style residence, designed by Philadelphia architect Samuel Sloan, has been a home for North Carolina governors since 1891.

Andy Griffith, the famous Tar Heel actor who probably is best-known as the sheriff of television's "Mayberry, R.F.D.," could find hundreds of towns like Mayberry tucked away in his home state. Country living is gracious and relaxed, affording the pleasures enjoyed by our grandfathers. Simple and picturesque homes abound; mountain streams remain a joy to fish; and there are country stores perched beside hundreds of crossroads where tall tales continue to be told around potbellied stoves as in years gone by.

Although the state is best known for its abundance of small and medium-sized towns, Charlotte is typical of the growing high-tech cities of the sunbelt. The Queen City's skyline (at left) reflects its rapid growth. With a population of over 300,000, the city is home of over 900 manufacturing companies, producing products ranging from chemicals to textiles. A banking center, it also boasts an opera company and symphony. As in other large cities, skilled computer-sophisticated employees are attracted by the more affluent lifestyles of the metropolis, sacrificing roomy rural living for the convenience of an apartment or townhouse in the suburbs, close to the workplace.

161

Small wonder tourism is a $3 billion industry in North Carolina. Outdoor dramas are a must for summer visitors seeking history served as entertainment. Real Cherokee Indians lend authenticity in Cherokee to Kermit Hunter's "Unto These Hills" (at left), which chronicles the tragic history of the tribe's struggle to retain their ancestoral lands in the mountains. Pulitzer Prize-winner Paul Green's outdoor drama about the first English colony in the New World draws thousands of visitors to "The Lost Colony" (below) in Manteo each year. And World War II comes to life again in Wilmington on the Cape Fear River for visitors to "The Immortal Showboat," the sound and light show at the USS North Carolina, photographed at right. The 35,000 ton battleship, which participated in every major Pacific offensive, was purchased by the state through a public fund-raising effort. It stands as a memorial to the men and women who served in the United States military in World War II.

There's a Mule Day at Benson, a National Hollerin' Contest at Spivey's Corner, a ramp convention at Waynesville. Tar Heels love festivals, whether they celebrate bluegrass music or tobacco. Festivals are a time for kicking up heels, making a little music and having fun. One of the most colorful festivals is the Grandfather Mountain Highland Games and Gathering of the Clans at Grandfather Mountain near Linville. Representatives of over 100 clans meet at the mountain each July for dancing and athletic contests as the skirl of bagpipe music mingles with the morning mist over the valley.

Recreation is year-round in our state's temperate climate. There are 350 golf courses in North Carolina, not all as famous as those sandhill courses at Pinehurst and Southern Pines but challenging nonetheless. The undulating fairways and emerald greens of the Hound Ears course (at left) near Blowing Rock make it both testing and beautiful. In winter, the snow-dusted mountain slopes sparkle in the sunlight like confectionery sugar. Then, thousands flock to the state's 11 ski resorts, attacking downhill runs like this one at Sugar Mountain resort at Banner Elk.

It's a gas! Whether you prefer the drone of gas-driven stockcars racing in NASCAR competition or the soft hiss of propane inflating hot air balloons for a race over the treetops, there's plenty to see on a sunny afternoon.

The National Balloon Rally, sponsored by the Statesville Chamber of Commerce, has been a three-day annual event in Statesville since 1973. About 100 balloonists from all over the country participate, and from 10,000 to 15,000 spectators attend this family oriented gala held in the fall to insure a "color spectacular."

The World 600 at the Charlotte Motor Speedway draws an interesting cross section of fans, from bank presidents to good ole boys fresh from the farm. Over 150,000 persons witnessed the World 600 in 1984, making it the number one spectator event in the state and one of the largest in the nation.

168

The usually gentle but consistent winds on the Carolina coast persuaded the Wright Brothers to choose Kitty Hawk as a place for their experiments with powered gliders. Small wonder, then, that Francis Rogallo, the developer of the hang glider, makes his home at Kitty Hawk, or that thousands have taken to the sport in the Old North State. Grandfather Mountain is also a favorite launching site for the gliders, offering a spectacular view over a mile high for those with enough daring. Those coastal winds are favorable for sailing, too. The shad boats the Wrights once viewed on the Albemarle Sound have disappeared, replaced by sportier sailing craft: windsurfers and catamarans.

172

There is a timeless quality about the land and water in that place that Thomas Wolfe called "Old Catawba." Indian words abound in the naming of places from Wanchese in the east to Hiwassee in the west. Near Mt. Pisgah, children slide the rush of water cascading over rocks as young braves must have done centuries before. The Nantahala River is now challenged by rafters instead of Indians in canoes. But the setting sun still puts an Indian eye over homes in the valley before disappearing behind the Great Smokies.

INDEX TO THE TIMELINE

ACKNOWLEDGEMENTS

Photography by
Joel Arrington
Outdoor Editor, N.C. Travel
& Tourism Division
Raleigh, N.C.
Pages 24, 26 left, 34, 145,
154.

Photography by
Diane Davis
Professional Photographer
Charlotte, N.C.
Pages 143 left, 169.

Photography by
James E. Eldridge
Professional Photographer
Hillsborough, N.C.
Page 12.

Photography by
Gene Furr
Photographer, The News and
Observer
Raleigh, N.C.
Pages 39, 45, 48, 50, 58, 147.

Photography by
Charles Gupton
Professional Photographer
Wake Forest, N.C.
Page 142.

Photography by
Chip Henderson
Professional Photographer
Raleigh, N.C.
Pages 2, 8, 13, 16, 20, 22, 25,
27, 143 right, 149, 150
bottom, 153, 155, 156, 158
bottom, 160 top, 161, 162
right, 168 left.

Photography by
Ray Matthews
Professional Photographer
Nags Head, N.C.
Page 171.

Photography by
Glenn Morris
Author & Photographer
Raleigh, N.C.
Pages 19, 32.

Photography by
Hugh Morton
President, Grandfather
Mountain
Linville, N.C.
Pages 14, 21, 138, 151, 158
top, 163, 164 left, 165,
170 top, 176.

Photography by
Clay Nolan
Photographer, N.C. Travel
& Tourism Division
Raleigh, N.C.
Pages 4, 6, 15, 18, 29, 145,
148 top, 150 top, 152, 157
160 bottom, 162 left, 164
right, 166, 172.

Photography courtesy
of North Carolina Division
of Travel and Tourism
Pages 148 bottom, 167.

Photography courtesy
of North Carolina
Nature Conservancy
Pages 23 bottom, 26 right.

Photography by
Pat Patterson
Professional Photographer
Raleigh, N.C.
Pages 31, 159.

Photography by
Nancy J. Pierce
Professional Photographer
Charlotte, N.C.
Page 168 right.

Photography by
Bruce Roberts
Senior Photographer,
Southern Living Magazine
Birmingham, Ala.
Pages 33, 42, 44, 129,
170 bottom, 173.

Photography by
Foster Scott
Professional Photographer
Nags Head, N.C.
Pages 38, 144.

Photography by
Ken Taylor
Photographer, Wildlife in
North Carolina Magazine
Raleigh, N.C.
Pages 17, 23 top, 28, 114, 146.

Photography by
John Warner
Professional Photographer
Black Mountain, N.C.
Page 30.

Illustrations by
Web Bryant
Pages 10, 37, 41, 47, 49, 51,
53, 55, 56, 61, 116, 119,
120, 122, 125, 127, 130,
132, 137, 140, 141.